A portion of your purchase of this book will go to support the James P. White Memorial Scholarship Endowment. This endowment preserves the legacy of Jim White, a 1989 Clemson graduate who died tragically in the terrorist attack on the World Trade Towers in 2001. Established by his parents and close friends in 2002, this endowment provides need-based scholarships to deserving Clemson students.

I have (had) enough

MEMOIRS OF ABUNDANCE IN FATHERHOOD, FRIENDSHIP, AND FAITH

JEFF JACOBSON

Dedication

I'm noticing that you don't have your own section in this book. You have the first chapter, but that doesn't seem quite enough. Then I realized you're always there, woven in and throughout everything I write because you are the fabric of this family. You're the one who holds us all together, but you don't do it alone because you're a prayer warrior. You're a hero to each of our children and you're mine too. You're that good angel on my right shoulder when a devil competes for attention on the left. These stories couldn't exist without you, so I dedicate this book to you, Kristie.

Ray & MaryAnn —
Hope you enjoy!
Much love,
Jeff Jacobson
2 Cor. 9:8

CONTENTS

FOREWORD

Ten random things you should know about me:

1. I married my best friend. She still is.
2. I follow Jesus.
3. Most of my favorite foods are really, really bad for me. I still eat them.
4. I would much rather write than talk.
5. I think my daughter is the most beautiful girl in the world and she smells like everything nice.
6. I think that my three sons will always be great friends, even if they don't smell as nice as their sister.
7. I wonder if Jesus thinks religious denominations are silly.
8. My oldest son is a Marine and I'm pretty proud of him. Hard not to be.
9. My middle two sons are twins, but they're as different as night and day.
10. I have had enough.

Part One

IT BEGINS

I'm new to marriage and the first Bush is president.
Pretty soon there is a child: my son.
Then there is infertility and I'm supposed to be learning
about God's timing.
After five years of this, there are two more boys, at the same
time. People ask us if twins run in our family,
and we say they do now.
Then there is a fourth: a girl.
Right before she is born, my best childhood friend dies
when planes fly into the Twin Towers.
I write a lot about all of this. These are my stories.

CHAPTER 1

The Hub of the Wheel

It's early autumn and Ronald Reagan has settled into his second term. On this day of consequence, I see her for the first time, leaning against a wall. Her hair is long, blonde, and sort of curly, and the light is shining through a window, bouncing from this to that and reflecting off her in a surreal, angelic way. I don't know it yet, but she will soon become the love of my life.

I also learn before long that she is good and virtuous and mostly naive, while I am not. She's unimpressed with the likes of me, but I try to convince and coax her to my side just the same. As beautiful on the outside as her inside is pure, somehow I know that she'll see right through me, right down into the center of me, and realize that I'm wild and irreverent and untamed—and mostly tarnished.

Sure enough, she does; yet, surprisingly, she stays.

And so it is that we grab onto each other for the days ahead of promise and joy, and that surreal sunlight-filled day in September turns into a year, and a year into thirty—years that defined, honed, and crafted us both. We have become best friends and we continue to beat the odds, aiming to be the one in two marriages that ends in marriage. There are no secret strategies, no books we've read on the subject. We simply share a love that burrows itself in as a steady tug of the spirit or a permanent but easy tap on the shoulder; it is a forward soul-momentum that approaches a speed where we have to clasp hands and negotiate turns and just hang on. Sometimes we lean back, close our eyes, and hold our breath until it's over.

Through it all, we nurture a shared language with origins in a secret place only we know. It is a certain type of romantic dialogue, I suppose, for, above the chaos and din of parenthood and responsibilities and adulthood in general, we hear each other without speaking. We've cultivated and perfected it over the years without even noticing, but our fluency allows us to acknowledge quick glances, recognize innuendo, and retreat into each other often. There, we occupy each other's space without sacrificing individuality.

My wife makes everything beautiful—it's just her way. She lights up a room, a day, or a life. In little and not-so-little ways, her personality, character, and smile alter moods and lift spirits. She is the mother of four and quite decidedly the hub of the wheel. She is the taskmaster and the coach who calls us in from the sidelines, grabs us by the shoulders, and tells us to get our heads in the game. She is literally a breath of springtime, a crashing wave of summer, a stunning mosaic fall kaleidoscope, and the dazzling purity of the first winter snow, all wrapped into one.

God knew our lives would be filled with glorious highs and rock-bottom lows and that our adventures would overflow with unparalleled wonder and magnificent colors. But He also knew that the only way we would ever find the fullness of grace and the sustenance to persevere would be if we were by each other's side. It would only happen through our oneness.

All these years later, it's true that she still sees right through me. I'd like to think that I'm a little less wild, perhaps more reverent, and certainly more tame. But it doesn't matter, because she loves me and accepts me for who I am. She has been intimately and intricately designed for such a time as this, prepared through the seasons and the chapters of her own life to join with mine. And I with hers.

And for us to tackle it together.

CHAPTER 2

My Friend Jimmy

It occurs to me that I grieve in small, acceptable amounts, such that are befitting a man, or at least a certain type of man. Far be it from me to mourn big and deep like one who's lost and helpless and, perhaps, desperate. No, not me. Instead, I bury my sadness away and take it out to acknowledge it from time to time; I examine it and appreciate it at arm's length, like I would an old family watch or a photo in a dusty scrapbook.

I'm not proud of my way—trust me—but it's all quite suitable for these masculine, ever-so-reserved emotions that I bear.

I say this because, shortly after the planes flew into the World Trade Center, my friend Jimmy lost all of his life. And while I didn't quite realize it at the time, I lost part of mine. I've been accepting this truth in tiny, tolerable doses ever since.

It just so happens that Jimmy was my best friend growing up, and so, just like childhood, memories of him will always be preserved in vivid color and stunning detail. We were the Huck and the Tom of Cranbury, New Jersey. The Millstone River ran through my backyard, and if you didn't know this already, rivers and boys are just about as perfect a combination as you could ever want. And so, adventures on the river nurtured a deep friendship that flowed through grade school, meandered into junior high, and rushed straight on into the rapids of high school.

Jimmy and I shared everything, as best friends do, and by everything I mean birthday parties and schemes and backyard forts and trouble. We ventured together into a certain coming of age and challenged head-on that awkward teenage angst; we enjoyed a love of the outdoors, sports, girls, and Springsteen concerts. He was with me for that first dance, that first beer, and maybe not too far away from that first anything.

When college came for both of us, we went our separate ways, and time and distance eventually caused the inevitable breaking away of a childhood bond. I was married early and became a father, but Jimmy believed in marrying a bit later, and so he was still dating and enjoying bachelorhood to the fullest while I was changing diapers.

Despite the difference of trajectory, we would still call each other on our birthdays and get caught up, usually at our respective jobs—his in some office high up in the World Trade Center and mine in some not-so-high office in Fort Wayne, Indiana.

Jimmy was an analyst with Cantor Fitzgerald, and so our conversations were often interrupted mid-sentence for him to scream something unintelligible at people around him. He worked on some sort of a bond trading floor, and I later learned that these orders involved the buying or selling of millions of dollars with just one shout. He probably had another phone on his other ear, but he would return to the conversation casually, never missing a beat, multi-tasking his way through the latest on life with his friend living halfway across the country. And so, the last time I spoke to Jimmy was on July 22, 2001. He turned thirty-four that day.

Jimmy was the oldest of five children, and with his job at Cantor he probably made more money in one year than I would make in twenty. He was one of the youngest limited partners in that company's history, and yet he drove a modest car and lived in a small apartment in New Jersey. He apparently devised other ways to spend his money, and so he helped with the graduate school tuition of his siblings because he, like his parents, believed strongly in their education. He often loaned his friends money, and he doted on his nieces and nephews with abandon. Jimmy's generosity and loyalty to his family and friends became the prevailing theme of what was remembered of him at his memorial.

I wrote a letter to Jimmy's parents after the terrorist's attack, and was honored when his father read part of it his memorial service:

"As most boys did, we often found ourselves in trouble. We were the masters of many schemes, and Jimmy was the natural leader of them all. He was the brave one, frequently defending me against whatever bully I had provoked. I remember vividly a time when Jimmy confronted a growling dog that was sprinting toward us. He stood face-to-face with this dog—unflinching—while I cowered behind him. The dog met his match and walked away without harm to either of us.

"Jimmy had a strength that cannot be described. He possessed a natural courage that created a steady, unwavering way about him. I remember, even as a child, knowing that he would always be a leader but at the same time a loyal and true friend."

Jimmy ran with the bulls in Spain and in the New York City Marathon, and he skied all over the world. He lived a large life and challenged himself on a regular basis. He literally exploded outward, not wanting to miss anything with the time he had.

With my knowledge of Jimmy, and from what I've gathered after the fact, there may have been some time after the planes struck that terrible morning, for people in his office to devise some type of escape plan. If one existed, Jimmy would have found it. But there would be no escape. All exits and paths downward were blocked, and moving upward was found early on to be for naught.

Jimmy was dating a girl from the office, and I remember seeing pictures later of a young professional couple jumping together from the smoke-filled building. It made me wonder because it wasn't a stretch for me to imagine him saying, "I will not cower and fade away in the smoke. I will not wait for a rescue that's never going to come."

And so, quite possibly, he grabbed the hand of the one he loved, and he died the same way that he lived, exploding outward and experiencing what was left of his life to the fullest.

Literally hundreds of Cantor Fitzgerald employees perished that day. After the debris was cleared, the only physical remainder found and given to Jimmy's parents was his charred driver's license, which gets me every time, because how could that be all that's left of such a life?

I write this many years later, because I guess this is just the way I grieve.

Moments have tumbled by, many with his memory caught up in the mix. And those memories are starting to pursue me and overtake me at times. I need to start sorting them out, because they're probably all bungled up and tangled now.

All of that to say, I guess I just wanted you to know a little something of my friend Jimmy. It's a tribute that's been a long time coming.

CHAPTER 3

The Daddy Cage

My little girl wandered into the room on the cutting edge of a fever. She didn't exactly know what she wanted, but she knew what felt right, so her head nestled snugly into my chest. Her hair smelled like everything nice.

Three older brothers tumbled into the room soon after with imaginations in full inclination, their accelerators jammed to the floor. It was a blur of dull swords and daring moves, battle cries and elbows, and the action veered much too close for my comfort. So my hand went out. They would *not* get close to her under my watch, especially when she was sick. She whimpered but knew that she was safe all at once.

Whether in sickness or health, scenarios like this played out often in the tumultuous world of three older brothers and one baby sister. The oldest was a strong leader, the judge and jury, not mild in any sense of the word. His adventures played hard and his younger twin brothers were never too far behind. Still, the princess poked her head into their world periodically to imagine and then declare that she was tougher than all of them. She raised her voice at them. She was my wife in a small body.

Should things not go her way, she would always run to me for protection, because she knew that she would get it.

Back to the moment at hand. I laid her down on the couch. Her skin was warm, and she was weak from the fever. My one-armed defense just wasn't working as the battle intensified before my very eyes. The big-brothers world of make-believe had no tolerance for a sick little sister.

So it was that I needed both arms to fight off those Tasmanian devils. I entered the melee on my knees and swept Levi away. I went right for the smallest of the three and captured him into a cage made only with my body. I positioned my joints and limbs in such a way that he'd never get out.

It was all big fun and they loved it. And it was my secret—and yours to keep now—that I loved this cage thing too, and I always will. I was more than eager to play because I got to swallow up my boys and hold them tight. I imagined it lasting forever. Maybe heaven is just like this, and there I wouldn't have to let them go.

But I digress.

Boys, being boys in the truest sense of the word, only wanted to break *out* of this literal man-made cage. Levi's brothers attempted rescues while there was great struggle beneath, complete with kicking and punching and gnashing of teeth. It was all to no avail until I relented to my benevolent spirit and let him escape.

And on a much healthier day, Chloe too wanted to be a part of this. Right about then, she was two or so and she entered the cage for the first time. She'd always been small for her age, long wavy hair with beautiful brown skin and thoughtful dark eyes. If she wanted to play in this rough-and-tumble world of father-son bonding, then so be it.

So I completely engulfed her. Only little bits of her blonde locks could be seen to an outsider. I remember taunting her to escape: "Chloe, you're in the daddy cage. I won't let you out!" I pulled my body in tight, ready for the struggle.

But there was nothing.

Tighter still, I cocooned her in with only a small window between a big arm and a leg. Surely she'd want an early release from this death trap.

"Chloe, you can't get out!"

Silence.

I leaned back to look at her. "Chloe, what's wrong?"

Quietly, she looked up at me as if I was from another planet. "I don't want to get out."

Huh? Well, that just wouldn't do. "She's not playing the game right," I announced to anyone who would listen. "You don't want to get out? Of course you do!" I teased. "I bet you can't!"

But there was nothing. My daughter just laid there like a rag doll, curiously content and curled up in a fetal position. Her eyes had closed.

What? How could this be? So I started to tickle her. She laughed only briefly.

"Daddy, cage again," she ordered.

I remember looking at her, baffled for a moment until it sunk in.

"Daddy, cage again," she said once more, letting me in on her worldview.

So that's what I did. I daddy-caged it again and she nestled in tighter, all snuggled as if in the safest place in the world.

CHAPTER 4

Don't Pick Up the Urinal Penny

Not long ago, while leaving to go on vacation, I set out to drive to my destination because I'm allergic to buying plane tickets for six people at once.

And so it was, in and out of those miles and through tunnels and over bridges, that I had *issues*. I'm not proud of them, trust me. But, alas, they were there.

Let me just spill it, for illustrative purposes, of course: If it were up to me, my children would never take bathroom breaks on long trips. I can hold it until I'm nearly internally damaged, and so should they.

The reason behind this is that I have problems with germs. Most importantly, I have trouble with the germs that I can't see but I know are in the public restrooms. Especially men's rooms, which are the ones I frequent. Even more troublesome are the men's public restrooms that pepper the highways and byways of this great nation of ours.

I don't think I'm alone in this.

So, you can imagine, as the journey pressed onward, I entered under extreme duress the latest version of a restroom for the fourth time in just as many hours as the trip had been underway.

When I gathered all of my courage, I went inside and stood a full body length away from the dreaded public urinal. I required my son Levi, the current cause of that particular stop, to do the same.

Yes, I know, most of it went on the floor, but at least we weren't stepping in anything that other fathers and their sons had left behind from when they only stood a half body's length away.

You see, then—and frankly, now—I can't step on anything near a urinal because I swear that something will get on my shoes and crawl up my pant leg. And then attack me in the minivan. A urinal to me is really just something to shoot for, not to embrace. But, all the same, there's a certain portion of our society that can sidle right up to the urinal and literally place itself in it. I believe 100 percent of four-year-old boys belong to that society. They just don't know any better, and a urinal is cool to them.

And so it was, on that day, that Levi, my four-year-old member of that society (forced against his will to stand a full body length away from the urinal), dropped the shiny new penny that he had just found. I don't know where he found it and, really, I didn't want to know. But the penny dropped and rolled in a perfect circle, round and round, and it came to rest smack dab in the danger zone of the urinal floor.

And, of course, he went to pick it up.

It's no exaggeration to say that I died a thousand deaths as he reached for it, and then I saved him from certain peril at the last possible moment. As I pulled him out of that man-made hell, I was screaming on the inside while Levi was screaming on the outside. I grabbed a paper towel to get the door because I couldn't touch the handle and Levi was putting bloody murder to words.

"That's my penny, Dad! I want my penny!"

The whole place was looking at him then, as I tried to explain that we don't want to pick up the urinal penny. I promised him over and over again that I'd get him another penny. Two pennies. Three shiny ones. Maybe even a dollar.

But something about that penny he had to have.

I let him down for a moment because he was all squirmy—
just a moment, mind you—so that I could buy some snacks and
drinks, and as I turned my attention to the cashier, Levi, the urinal lover, made a run for it back toward the cesspool, just to get
his hands on that crazy penny.

"I want my penny, Daaadddd!"

I bolted after him, quickly fumbling through the change the
cashier gave me, looking for just the right amount of currency to
take his mind off that one friggin' cent.

He exploded through the restroom door and made a turn
toward the abomination, and he was almost in a head-first dive as
I scooped him up (to save his life again) just in the nick of time.
Grown men who were previously in the bathroom with me were
laughing and pointing and telling the story to their wives and
friends.

With Levi in my right arm, kicking and screaming and mourn-
ing his loss, I hauled him out to the van, penniless and heartbro-
ken. In my left arm, I clutched the snacks and drinks that would
ironically pass right through him and my other children, in and
out of miles and through tunnels and over bridges, so that I'd have
the great fortune of visiting yet another roadside public restroom.

As we finally drove away, I thought long and hard about how
amazing it was that Levi didn't grasp the putrescence and the
germs. Even though they crawl and seek to devour little boys and
grown men like me, he didn't care.

But I am Levi in a big man's body, and something about *that*
penny I must have. It is priceless to me even though I have a
Father who knows it is worthless and He has promised me better.
I keep going back when I think His back is turned. I'm screaming
and kicking and making my way to the shiny thing, not recogniz-
ing the filth and foul of the public restroom floor that is my pride.
Things that are so valuable to me, when put in the context of this
Levi story and his urinal penny, become a lot less so. In small and
not-so-small ways, I start to see what I'm being offered instead.

He has said He'll multiply my pennies. Two pennies. Three shiny ones. Maybe even a dollar. It's a whole pocket full of pennies and wealth of a different sort.

It's a promise of abundance and to be vibrantly alive.

CHAPTER 5

Levi's Doomed Tooth

One afternoon when the Jacobson kids were little, I met my wife, Kristie, at the dentist's office. The kids were there for their bi-annual visit. When I arrived, she had some errands to run, so away she went.

As I sat there flipping through a magazine, various hygienists emerged to update me on a particular child, each encouraging me with news of stellar check-ups.

Well . . . except for Levi's hygienist, that is.

She emerged to advise me in the gravest tone possible that Levi had his first cavity and politely asked if it would be all right for him to come back the very next day for his filling. I proceeded to schedule his return visit while the kids picked out a toy or a new toothbrush. Then we loaded up in the minivan for the ride home.

Now, having myself grown up with an older sister who was mostly a nurturer, I had no frame of reference for what would soon transpire for Levi, who is, in fact, navigating life with older brothers who are mostly torturers.

Gabe, the eldest, started in first and told Levi that a cavity meant the dentist was going to have to rip the tooth right out of his head. Tate added (for kicks) that before he ripped it out of his head, the dentist was going to hit it with a hammer a few times to knock it loose. Trying to keep up, Chloe, the youngest, chimed in and said it was gonna hurt, big time.

And so Levi smacked her, just because.

After I told Levi to never hit a girl, I told him not to listen to anything his evil siblings were saying. But, as you may suspect, the damage was already done. After a few moments of strained silence, I looked in the rearview mirror and saw that a holy terror had settled upon Levi's face, the likes of which I'd never seen. Trying hard not to cry, he looked out the window as if his young life was passing before his very eyes.

Later that night, while enduring a not-so-peaceful dinner with the torturers and the tortured, the subject of Levi's doomed tooth and its need for a filling resurfaced. While I had sensed in the car that the worst was over, I had grossly underestimated the resources the torturers still possessed. Their consensus was that Levi would need laughing gas to survive this procedure.

Attempting to stop this conversation in its tracks, and unknowingly taking leave of my senses, I said that Levi did *not* need laughing gas, because it's about $70 for a whiff of it, it's not covered by dental insurance, and I've never needed it, so why should Levi?

Then Gabe said that without the laughing gas, when they rip the tooth out of Levi's head, it's not gonna be funny at all. Tate brought up the hammer again.

Levi took a swing at poor Chloe before she could even open her mouth.

By then we all knew what was coming next. Levi does this thing where he's not quite crying but he starts to rub his eyes. While he was desperately attempting to stave off the inevitable, I tried to put my finger in the dike.

"Levi, don't listen to anyone. It'll be fine," I said. "No one is going to pull a tooth out of your head or hit it with a hammer." And then, taking further leave of my senses, I blubbered, "They're going to give you a shot of Novocain. You won't feel a thing."

Within a nanosecond of it leaving the tip of my tongue, a quick side glance at my wife confirmed that any reference to any type of shot was cause for another type of disaster.

Sure enough, Gabe, the head torturer, said that the shot wasn't the worst part of it all and it would only get worse without the laughing gas because now Levi would have the shot and then the dentist would rip the tooth out of his head. Before Tate could even weave his own tortuous hammer tale, the dam broke and Levi started to cry. As the crying reached a crescendo, Tate thought that maybe a hammer at this point was too harsh, so he brought up the drill instead.

Right then I knew that I would be purchasing a $70 whiff of nitrous oxide for an eight-year-old boy the very next day.

●　●　●

Later the next evening, as he was vigorously brushing his teeth, I asked Levi how it went. He said it didn't hurt at all. Kristie, who had sat by his side, said he giggled through the whole thing.

CHAPTER 6

I Shouldn't Have to Tell You

I shouldn't have to tell you again how much I love you, so this time I won't.

But I will pull your older brother aside and tell him to keep a close eye on you at school.

I will take away texting if it helps you study. I will take away *everything* if it helps you study.

I will put my hand on your chest tonight, while you're sleeping, to make sure you're still breathing.

I will watch your practice from the sidelines as you get tackled harder than you've ever been tackled before.

I will stay on the sidelines this time and let you work it out on your own, even when I can tell you're crying inside your helmet.

I will make you put on your seat belt. Again.

I will plunge the toilet. Again.

I will tell you to wash your hands. I will tell you to brush your teeth. I will tell you to not run and fight with your siblings while the toothbrush is still in your mouth

I will leave the door open a crack when you go down into the basement with your girlfriend.

I will never let your sister go in the basement with a boyfriend.

I shouldn't have to tell you again how much I love you, so this time I won't.

But I will tell you to get a job the next time (and every time) you ask for money.

I will get up in the morning and go to my job.

I will take better care of myself.

I will assign you chores and you will do them, or you will not eat.

I will not pick up after you again.

I will let you have a sleepover with all your hungry friends. Again.

I will play Old Maid with you and make sure I end up with the Old Maid. Again.

I will be the audience for your made-up dance routines and watch as you twirl everything in the house that resembles a baton.

I will make you look your coach or your teacher in the eye when you're being disciplined. I will make sure you know that I know that most of the time you deserve it.

I will grab you when you walk by and I'll hold you close into my chest and I'll breathe in the smell of your hair on the top of your head while you're still shorter than me, just one more time, while I still can.

I will pray that you end up a lot more like Jesus and a lot less like some Christians.

I shouldn't have to tell you again how much I love you, so this time I won't.

But I will remind you again and again that we're a family and we always stick together.

I will allow you to fiercely protect your siblings.

I will let you fight your siblings periodically so that you actually know how to fiercely protect your siblings.

I will turn off the TV and take away your cell phones and anything else electronic and we will play Scrabble.

I will take you to a noun called church but teach you how to be a verb called Church.

I will only allow two kids on the trampoline at one time. I will now dismantle the trampoline because you're not listening to me.

I will tell your mother how much I love her and then I'll kiss and hug her in front of you. Again and again and again.

I will drive you to school. Again. I will drive you to practice. Again. I will drive you to get your favorite sub. Again.

I will try hard to remember again what life was like when I was your age.

I shouldn't have to tell you how much I love you, but just this last time I will. Again.

CHAPTER 7

A Love There is No Cure For

So, it's important to care about the poor and it's equally important to show our kids that we care about the poor, so that maybe they'll eventually care too. And not just care but *love* with authenticity like it's natural and a normal part of their existence.

I write this because there was a homeless man living in the alleyway downtown and I wanted to bring him a tarp because it was going to rain. Gabe, who was a bit younger (in fifth grade) at the time, came with me on this adventure.

When we arrived, I slowly weaved my car in between narrow houses and ultimately to the place where I had last seen the homeless man in the alleyway of a deserted movie theater called the Rialto. Gabe's eyes grew big because it was early in the evening, and it was shadowy down there, looking like something out of Dante's imagination with broken bottles and overgrown weeds and evidence of what happens when the light doesn't quite reach certain spaces. I realized alleys are scary to kids, but I got out of the car quickly, naturally, and acting as though I was not as afraid as maybe I should have been. Gabe stayed in the car and watched from the window. He yelled out, "Be careful," something he'd never said—ever—so I glanced back quickly. He looked like he was truly scared for me, like I was going to find my doom in there or something.

I walked all the way to the end and, wouldn't you know it, the homeless man was gone. No blankets, no sign of him whatsoever. I was sad because I had missed my chance to help this man and have my son witness it. So I walked back to the car and explained that he was gone.

As the words were leaving my mouth, I began to wonder if I had planned to help him so that Gabe could witness it or if I wanted to help him just to help him. I didn't have to wonder long because Gabe immediately asked why I hadn't helped him and why I had waited until now and why I hadn't done more.

Lacking answers, I decided to drive around to the front of that vacant broken-down theater. We looked up at the empty marquee together. Gabe was just starting up a band, so we imagined what it might look like someday with his band's name in lights up there. Back then he was going to be a drummer, not the U.S. Marine he eventually became.

I asked him what kind of music they would play and he said redemptive rock. I think he had heard me use that term. He wanted to know what kind of music that was, and I told him he'd know it when he found it. We talked a little about redemption and how it's a little like what Jesus does, or maybe a lot like it. He agreed that maybe this would be a good kind of music for his band to play.

We drove just a little farther to turn down a side street called Taber so that maybe we could salvage this educational trip and meet a new Somali Bantu refugee family that had arrived on Friday. No one was outside, though, and all the doors were closed and I thought it might be offensive to just knock on their door without calling. So I kept driving.

When we were some distance from their house, I looked in the rearview mirror and five or six Somali children spilled out of the front door and ran into the yard wearing African garb. It was just like when a flock of birds erupts from a cornfield all at once. It was beautiful like that. We had just missed them, but we were on a one-way street, so we kept going.

Heading home toward our comfortable southwestern suburb, I went to put in some Springsteen but couldn't find any. So I threw in something else—the Partridge Family. Now I don't need to tell you what a sacrilege this is, to go from The Boss to David Cassidy, but despite my preference for the former, there the latter was. And, you know, it was that song where David Cassidy thinks he loves me.

And so, windows went down and we sang together, for our entire town to hear, our version of the words: "We think we love you, even though we're afraid that we're not sure of, a love there is no cure for."

You remember the song.

And it struck me then, deep down where profound things sneak in and grab hold, that maybe my eyes—and by default, Gabe's too—were only seeing the things that were temporary, not the unseen that is eternal. I was protecting him, forcing him to stay in the car and watch a show. Come to think of it, maybe this whole thing was for show, a privileged father manufacturing a moment or two for his son to see, a forced encounter meant only to offer a taste of a different side of life.

What am I so afraid of, driving down these one-way streets of life, staring at missed opportunities? Why didn't I circle around for another pass? Why didn't I come down sooner to help this man who lived in the shadows of the Rialto?

Why, why, *why*?

That warning to be careful struck a unique chord that day. I imagined Gabe saying, "Be careful what you show me, Dad. Show me what it means to love. Don't just put on a show."

We live and breathe and go to extra lengths to truly love with authenticity that's deep and worn like a garment throughout our day and into our nights, in our comings and our goings. We long for a life and a love there is no cure for, because in the eternal wisdom of that redemptive rock song from the Partridge Family, isn't that what life is made of?

Maybe, just like David Cassidy, that's what I'm so afraid of.

CHAPTER 8

I Have Enough

I live in a place where I can worship the God I want to, when I want to, and where I want to. I go to a church that's about two minutes away, where I can ask forgiveness from that very same God for what I am about to write in this impromptu essay.

I have enough.

I can get out of bed and stand on my own two feet in the morning and begin to walk with only limited pain in my joints. I can breathe in and out. I am healthy, for the most part.

But, you see, it's just that my children, each of whom I love with the intensity of a thousand suns, well, they paint me three coats of crazy, drain my bank account, fight like cats and dogs, and drive me to drink. Fortunately, they too are healthy and have great potential to take care of me when I'm not so healthy and I'm unable to stand on my own two feet.

Speaking of cats and dogs, I have one of each and I look into their gentle eyes and I stroke their soft fur because my doctor says it will lower my blood pressure. I've been stroking their fur a lot lately, so they're getting a little bald behind the ears.

I have enough.

I have a house with four walls and a roof. But those walls are closing in on me now because these kids are getting so big and they're all pushing me out of my space until I'm left cowering and whimpering in the fetal position in some dark corner of a closet where they'll never find me. I come home from work with one nerve left and, instead of stepping on it, they yank it out and play jump rope with it.

I have enough.

Because, thank God, the summer of 2011, with its revolving door of sleepovers and teenagers and pre-teenagers, is finally over.

It's not a sleepover anyway. It's a *stay-up-all-night-and-sleep-at-first-light-over* with friends passed out on various couches or various floors around my house after they've decided to stay up on a Tuesday or Wednesday watching idiotic horror movies, while I'm upstairs having a fitful sleep wondering what they're doing downstairs, devising ways that I can become their own personal horror movie that goes a little something like this:

When morning comes, and I get ready for work, I will wander downstairs and find them all sleeping like little angels. I will pour ice cold water on their heads while I let rip what's left of the air horn we bought for last year's football season into their snuggly little ears. After I assume the role of their own personal alarm clock from hell, I will rouse them from their deep, dreamy slumber, and as they jump to attention, I will make each of them drop and give me twenty. Then I will order one of them to make me my coffee and another to go out and get me my paper. After that, I will send all of them out without breakfast to weed my mulch beds before the sun gets too hot, and I'll remind them there's a hose out there if they get thirsty. If they're not up for that, I will show them the front door and will tell them to get a job or find some form of a life that doesn't entail me working forty hours a week to support it, and then, lastly, I'll remind them I'm not running a shelter over here, and I'll order all of them to start sleeping in their own friggin' beds, in their own friggin' houses, for God's sake, and stop clinging to each other like a bunch of little girls holding hands on the kindergarten playground.

Whew. Dear God, so sorry for that.

I have enough.

I have running water and indoor plumbing. Carpet covers my floors. I have a carpet shampooer too, by the way, for all the times my darling children go to shake the orange juice without checking whether the top is on, or when the dog and the cat with gentle eyes and soft fur puke all over it.

Oh, and speaking of indoor plumbing, if I have to get out that plunger one more time, I swear to #*&$*#&.

I have vehicles to drive that are in relatively good shape.

Or at least they were before *you* started driving. You know who you are, Gabriel. Somehow I managed to drive the car you're now using for six years without incident, but in the last three months, you've tripled my insurance premiums, doubled my gas bill, taken out both side mirrors (on separate occasions, mind you), blown a tire and two rear speakers, added untold dents and scratches (one from hitting the side of the garage), blown bizarre fuses that I didn't even know existed, and came home one morning with exactly one-half of the vehicle covered completely in mud. I still haven't figured out how you did that, but I hope the guys from CSI don't show up looking for DNA.

I have enough.

The pantry is full of food, and there are leftovers in the refrigerator. There is food all over the place, in fact, because my children don't clean it up. For example, the shredded cheese from their homemade cheese wraps. They say the kitchen is clean, but they really haven't cleaned it. They've just contained something less than a disaster in the hopes I won't notice.

Here's a thought, children: when you and your friends are having a not-sleep-over and you decide to make cheese wraps with shredded cheese, a good start would be to get the actual cheese into the wrap so that I don't find what you *didn't* put in the wrap somewhere else, like on the floor, the countertops, and in the silverware drawers. What do you think I am, a big mouse that you're going to catch when I come down in the morning?

I have had enough! I mean, *I have enough.*

Despite my numerous issues, my wife still loves me after many years of marriage. I better double check that one. My parents and my big sister are alive and well, and they still love me too (I think), which is no small thing. I still have friends who love me and find great entertainment in my issues. I have a lot of issues if you couldn't tell.

I have a job. My wife has a job.

My teenage son has a job. Praise Jesus from whom all blessings flow. He cleans up after horses in a barn, and if karma is even remotely a real thing, every parent of a teenager will be nodding in agreement with a smug smile like mine, thinking that *this* irony, in and of itself, is more than enough.

College football is about to start, and Notre Dame is looking good.

The nights are getting cooler.

School is back in session.

There is order in the universe again.

I know that God forgives me for this, and therefore . . .

I have enough.

CHAPTER 9

When is Mom Coming Home?

My wife travels a lot these days. She's gone a night or two a week, which leaves me to manage the comings and goings of a house full of kids. Or, I guess you could say I manage to get by, which is code for the kids manage not to starve.

Shortly after Kristie leaves on a trip, I hear three questions at various intervals. The first is, "When is Mom coming home?" The second is, "Where are we ordering pizza from tonight?" The last is, "When is Mom coming home again?" The first and the last are repeated with more insistence as time wears on. I try not to take it personally. Even as they ask it, I feel like the pathetic guy whose girlfriend is breaking up with him after a string of bad dates. Their eyes are kind, as if trying to soften the blow with, "It's not you. It's me."

I'm not a bad father. They just want their mom, who is much better at this sort of thing, which is code for everything. Teenagers need a personal assistant to navigate life. Not only for their schedules, but for their psyches. They need emotional support and moms are naturals at this.

Kristie is nurturing and calm and reassuring, and I'm, well . . . not. My default reaction is to tell them to figure it out themselves.

For example, in the morning, I know how to point them toward bowls, spoons, and cereal boxes. At lunch, they're on their own. When it's dinnertime, see the second question above. Lately, I've been making them call in the pizza order too. They've got to learn how to do it at some point, right?

Aside from the nutritional and emotional nourishment they're *not* getting from me, it's clear that when I'm not paying attention, which is often, my wife is still parenting via texting or FaceTime from a hotel room in some distant place. She's not a hovering helicopter mom; the kids are the ones going to *her*. They've learned to bypass me. I wouldn't be surprised if they set up secret group texts to make fun of me, like when I've fallen asleep on the couch—again—trying to stay awake through a game of Words with Friends.

Chloe: "Mom, he's snoring. It's only 5:30."

Kristie: "We're playing Words with Friends. It makes him fall asleep. He just played 'AT' so I know he's not very sharp right now."

Adding insult to injury, she'll even help with their homework through FaceTime, usually after I bark something from the couch like, "Do it yourself! No one ever helped me!"

As bedtime approaches, which is more of a theoretical thing when I'm in charge, I'm reminded that my wife does a better job with this too. When she's home, she has this annoying habit of talking with them, you know, face-to-face, making sure they have what they need for the next day, checking the laundry, and all that stuff. Then she goes into each of their bedrooms right before they go to sleep to pray with them.

When it's just me, I scream from downstairs to collect the garbage and do the dishes and clean out the litter box. If I do happen to see them all in one place before bed, I tell them to huddle up around me on the recliner, so we can do a group prayer while the game is paused. If you were on the outside looking in, you'd think they were laying hands on me.

At this part of the story, especially if you're a mom, you're probably thinking I deserve all of this because I'm such an irresponsible and non-nurturing father. I agree with you, which is why, right about then, I turned to Levi and asked . . .

"When is Mom coming home?

Now, before you think too little of me, I will share tha
get involved in a puking incident last night. There are some
a father is good for, especially *this* father; I have a very part
set of skills that I've acquired over the years. Kristie was a
ing machine when she was pregnant. I've cleaned up more v
from more places than anyone should ever have to describe. I
took a toilet apart once to clean up puke bits that went ev
where except for the actual round hole with water in it.

Anyhow, as you can imagine, Chloe was upstairs FaceTim
her mother, telling her that she was about to throw up. Instead
using the toilets on the second floor and figuring it out herself, s
decided she should pause her conversation long enough to con
downstairs and announce to me that she was about to throw up
She was speaking of it in a pleasant tone, as if a friend was goin
to stop by.

Levi was at the kitchen table doing some homework (that I
wouldn't help with), and he said, "Chloe, you never throw up.
You just *tell* everyone that you're going to throw up."

Well, last night she *did* throw up. Into the kitchen sink (with
all the dirty dishes that hadn't been put in the dishwasher) mostly
full of empty glasses. It kept coming and coming, so she was
essentially filling each glass with liquid pizza. Between heaves she
said that she wasn't sick, she was just throwing up because a boy
named Caleb gave her a bad cookie at school. She knew it was
Caleb's cookie because her friend Nadia also ate one and she was
throwing up too.

I kicked into gear as The Compassionate Father. I told her I
was sorry, and I pulled her hair back, rubbed her shoulders, and
then got her a cool cloth. After she was all done, I got her situated
upstairs so she could finish FaceTiming with her mother, who
obviously got the better end of the deal while I went back downstairs to deal with the puke. I started pouring it out of glasses
that were even more colorful because of what could have been the
cookie.

At this part of the story, especially if you're a mom, you're probably thinking I deserve all of this because I'm such an irresponsible and non-nurturing father. I agree with you, which is why, right about then, I turned to Levi and asked . . .

"When is Mom coming home?

Now, before you think too little of me, I will share that I did get involved in a puking incident last night. There are some things a father is good for, especially *this* father; I have a very particular set of skills that I've acquired over the years. Kristie was a puking machine when she was pregnant. I've cleaned up more vomit from more places than anyone should ever have to describe. I even took a toilet apart once to clean up puke bits that went everywhere except for the actual round hole with water in it.

Anyhow, as you can imagine, Chloe was upstairs FaceTiming her mother, telling her that she was about to throw up. Instead of using the toilets on the second floor and figuring it out herself, she decided she should pause her conversation long enough to come downstairs and announce to me that she was about to throw up. She was speaking of it in a pleasant tone, as if a friend was going to stop by.

Levi was at the kitchen table doing some homework (that I wouldn't help with), and he said, "Chloe, you never throw up. You just *tell* everyone that you're going to throw up."

Well, last night she *did* throw up. Into the kitchen sink (with all the dirty dishes that hadn't been put in the dishwasher) mostly full of empty glasses. It kept coming and coming, so she was essentially filling each glass with liquid pizza. Between heaves she said that she wasn't sick, she was just throwing up because a boy named Caleb gave her a bad cookie at school. She knew it was Caleb's cookie because her friend Nadia also ate one and she was throwing up too.

I kicked into gear as The Compassionate Father. I told her I was sorry, and I pulled her hair back, rubbed her shoulders, and then got her a cool cloth. After she was all done, I got her situated upstairs so she could finish FaceTiming with her mother, who obviously got the better end of the deal while I went back downstairs to deal with the puke. I started pouring it out of glasses that were even more colorful because of what could have been the cookie.

CHAPTER 10

This Is My House, Boy

So I have this ritual. I arm wrestle each new teenage friend who my sons bring through the door. I do this the first time they come over, especially if this friend has plans to eat my food, sleep in my basement, and essentially take up my space. They travel in packs, these kids, so I usually have a few to take on, one after another. Some who have previously tried (and failed) will return, looking for a rematch. Either way, they'll line up at the kitchen countertop, one by one, look me in the eye, and grab my hand for the challenge.

Despite their collective self-assurance, I can tell by the way each locks his hand with mine that I will win. It never fails. I have some strength left in this right arm of mine, but mostly I have experience on my side. These punks have little to none.

Once we begin, there's a valiant effort, adrenaline pumping through clean, unclogged teenage arteries. For the most part, these kids are strong. Veins pop on foreheads as they flex their muscular arms—arms that look a lot like mine used to.

Early in the match, I'll let each force my hand down within inches of the countertop. I love the look on each shiny face. Most believe that it's just about over. Such confidence and bravado each one possesses to think he's won, even though I remain unbeaten. Well, except for the three-hundred-pound linebacker from the football team a few years back. That wasn't fair, so should it tarnish my record? In fact, I think it was rigged.

The eventual panic sets in when I start to push back a little. I remind my young opponent that I'm old and out of shape. I also point out, in case he's forgotten, that his friends are watching. Right about then he'll look down and lean his shoulder into it, focus harder, and grit his teeth. Then he'll scream a mighty scream while his hand starts sweating, and I'll say, "Look me in the eye, boy. This is *my* house." Sometimes that alone is the beginning of the end.

Slowly I turn my wrist as leverage takes over and his friends start jeering. I'll ask him to tell everyone in the room who the man is (loud enough so my wife can hear too). Then, ever so slowly, over the top I go, watching the straining, the refusal, the desperate last-ditch effort, the gradual relenting, and finally, the humiliating defeat as it transforms the countenance of a once cocky face.

One of my sons usually saunters over right about then (after I've wrestled three or four challengers in a row) with his own last-ditch effort to capitalize on my fatigue, which he should know by now is for naught. Sometimes he's brave enough to do it in front of a girlfriend, but I don't back down. I hear emasculation builds character.

Now, you're probably thinking one of two things at this point. A.) That's mean, Jeff. You should be ashamed of yourself, or B.) Good for you, Jeff. Show 'em who's boss. Teach those boys some *respect.*

I honestly don't know why I do it. Some crazy tradition I started to get some testosterone flowing and celebrate feats of strength. I'll admit it feels good to know I can still win at my age, so maybe I do it to teach that experience and maturity can edge out sheer strength and audacity. Perhaps I do it because I desire to be a true friend to my sons and their friends, all the while clearly demonstrating the authority I have over them. Lord knows I don't want to regress and try to fit back into their group some other way, but I suppose everyone wants to be relevant and worthy of respect, right? These are hard to come by in the eyes of a teenager.

As desperate as it may sound, I think I'm just trying to connect, to be included and to grab onto them, even just for a moment. I'm out of touch with their motives and their rhythms; I don't speak their language and I'm not cool anymore. With this simple ritual, though, I'm briefly welcomed into their circle and given a nod of deference and approval from my sons. "The old man doesn't get beat," they'll say, before they escape into the basement or into a car. Into a world where I'm no longer welcome.

So, all of that to say, I'll keep arm wrestling these guys, maybe connecting a little by looking in their eyes and grabbing onto their hands for as long as they'll let me.

Maybe I don't need a reason. After all, it is my ritual.

And *my* house, *boy*.

CHAPTER 11

Love is Hard Work

Love doesn't need chocolates or candy hearts or big stuffed bears that take up room because . . .

Love takes up room. Love competes for room.

Love commiserates. Love forms a team.

Love encourages. Love affirms.

Love knows when to shut up and just do the dishes. Or . . .

Love turns off the game and listens.

Love becomes . . . *present.*

Love is the swallowing of opinions, and yet . . .

Love shares the truth.

Love is looking on the bright side, or, if needed . . .

Love embraces the dark side (because the bright side can be too cheery right about now).

Love ignores and love tolerates.

Love sits in silence.

No, wait . . . Love speaks up!

Love defends. Love carries a banner. Love is a crusader!

Love knows no boundaries. Except when there are . . . boundaries.

Love cries a little and love even weeps.

Love is stoic, sometimes, but love isn't weak.

Love knows how to keep its distance, retreat and reform.

Love calibrates. Love re-calibrates.

Love takes on giants, together, and then love prays the giants away.

Love shields. When all else cowers and shivers and shakes, love stands tall, unwavering.

Love protects. Love is a hero.

Love feels like a sprint at first, but love reveals it is a marathon. Love is a triathlon.

Love is an Ironman triathlon.

Love doesn't leave. Love doesn't stray. Even a little.

Love is a secret language.

Love is hard work.

Love isn't a holiday. Love isn't one day.

Love is what endures when everything else is gone.

Love remains.

CHAPTER 12

When the Sirens Cry Out

Everyone knows the sound of an ambulance siren. But when the sirens cry out, do you know how we *feel*?

Do you know that we drop everything and frantically look for our phones? That we count our blessings when we come to our senses and remember that you're asleep upstairs, or you're in the basement, or you're just down the street with a friend? If you're not, do you understand why we call and wait breathlessly until we hear your voice? You laugh and tell us not to worry, but . . .

When the sirens cry out, do you know how we feel?

It's a gut-wrenching moment. Yes, we know it's a miracle that you're ours—and that you're really God's—so each day is a blessing. Each day is another that you're here. You're not the one who the sirens were for, even as someone, somewhere, dropped everything just like we did, and they called, and they waited, and their nightmare was real.

You see, we've given everything for you: our youth, our energy, and our resources. And every penny, every strained nerve and stressed muscle, every worrisome moment has been worth it. It's just that you made us who we thought we could never become. So . . .

When the sirens cry out, do you know how we feel?

You can't possibly know. Someday, though, maybe. And when that someday comes, when someone you really love in an unexplainable way is out and about and you hear the sirens, you'll finally experience our reality. You'll know instinctively that something isn't right and the hairs on your arm will straighten a bit. It will wake you in the night.

He'll be your son. She'll be your daughter.

For now, just know that what we feel is a breath away from chaos. It's as close as we get to the edge of a canyon without falling in. The siren cries out for a reason. People just like you break, and accidents happen. You're not as invincible as you think, so . . .

When the sirens cry out, do you know how we feel?

It means everything to us that you're safe. Maybe you're not always happy, or maybe you're angry about this or that. But when we call, in that crucial moment, we just need to know that you're alright.

We just do.

We give you to God, once, twice, and again. Over and over we whisper a prayer, but it's still there. It's always there. We're your parents, so just do as we say and . . .

Please don't make the sirens cry out.

CHAPTER 13

I Am What I Drive

Someone, somewhere said that I am what I drive. This makes sense to me.

I drive a 2002 Honda Accord.

My car has a lot of miles on it. I think like a hundred and forty gazillion to be exact. There are scrapes and bumps and scars all over it, mostly caused by my kids. The check-engine light has been on for years, and I don't know why but I'm afraid to check (everything seems fine).

The paint job is a little lackluster but still salvageable, should I choose to buff it out.

But I probably won't.

You can see where I'm going with this. I tell my kids all about my six-pack. It's still there. It's salvageable. Maybe buried under the scrapes and bumps and scars (and mileage) of life. I just need to buff it out.

But I probably won't.

My Honda has a spoiler on the back. Yeah, I know. Seems stupid but it's for drag and lift and . . . oh, *forget* it. Who am I kidding? It's just for show. It's the equivalent of me wearing a tie and taking notes at a corporate team-building exercise. Some things are just for show.

It's a two-door. Seemed fine when the kids were little. They thought it was an adventure. But now? Now it's an embarrassment. My kids are embarrassed by my car. My kids are embarrassed by . . .

Yeah, I know.

You should appreciate that my Accord is a male car, so there's no calling it a *she*. Mostly I'll refer to my car as an *it* until I get emotional. And then it's definitely a *he*. I don't want my car to feel emasculated.

My Honda Accord has a sunroof. I only open it at night, so it's really a moonroof and the reason I don't open it during the day is because well . . . *skin cancer*. My car and I care about this, and responsibilities being what they are, we can't take any chances.

It has a six-cylinder, so it has something under the hood to remind others that it's pretty powerful. Or it can be with a tune-up. It still has some muscle, in an efficient sort of way (see my arm wrestling stories).

It's not an unattractive car. Well, I suppose it is. But in just the right light, there are glimpses of what it once was. The interior is clean but worn. You can't cover up weathering.

It can go fast for short distances. Then it starts to shake. And it leaks (let's not go there). Can you blame it?

Still, it's dependable. It starts in the morning, for the most part. It makes the commute, day after day (after day). It can get you from here to there. It's that kind of loyalty, over and over again.

Honestly, I look at your car and what it says about you and I'm jealous. You've obviously done something more impressive than I have, which is great. I'm happy for you. What my Honda says about me is that I have four kids, three going to college in the span of the next six years. My car whispers to me that I don't pay for him (yeah, I just switched from *it* to *him*); he's a friend to me because he doesn't want anything. He's long been paid for.

I don't want or need anything else. I'm okay with what I drive. If my car matters that much to you, then you probably like cars a whole lot.

I drive a worn out, dependable car with a lot of mileage.

This makes sense to me.

CHAPTER 14

And He Will Last

It's winter again and I've lost my energy. I'm not sure where it went. Maybe it checked out on me and caught the last train for the coast and it's prancing around in some sun-drenched town, shopping maybe, or riding a bike. It's laughing at me while I'm stuck here in Indiana, with its fickle weather and its muddy fields lined with lifeless trees, each of them overexposed with shadows of gray and brown.

So I need a good sunrise to wake me up—the soft kind, tinged with orange and purple and even cottony pink, with some vivid blues thrown in for good measure; the sort of spectacular sunrise that unexpectedly warms the room and lifts my spirits before I even throw back the curtain or lift the shades, promising something better to come, maybe April or May.

And when it arrives, I won't turn away because I know if I stare, it will last. If I turn away, thirty seconds will turn into a minute and a minute will become five, and when I look back it will be gone.

Now I know this kind of sunrise is explained away by some left-brain scientist as merely light coming up on the horizon, a perfect blend of reflected or absorbed or refracted sunlight through clouds and hazy polluted air, with geologic dust and an untold number of electrically charged particles all mixed together with atmospheric conditions to bring a stunning but fleeting reflection to my eyes.

Or, it could be God.

You see, science may not lie, but He has been known to turn ugly things pretty, just like He does with me (and maybe you) every day. We're not that far off from that polluted geologic dust that needs just the right blend of something to bring a stunning but fleeting reflection to the eyes of someone watching us.

I somehow need to remember that, because I'd much rather wander through the hopelessly muddy fields of winter, forgetting that I'm with you, and him, and her, all year long in fact, and that we're supposed to be the ones who multiply and form that untold number, the ugly pieces of nothingness coming together to become that very spectacular thing—the electrically charged particles of grace who are joining and serving and binding ourselves to the least of these, recognized as beautiful merely because of the Light that is shining through, from behind and the sides and straight down the middle of us.

We were meant to be that unexpected sunrise that warms the room and lifts spirits, the kind that promises something better to come, with beauty that no one would ever want to turn away from, because Someone is being reflected, coming up behind us on the horizon, and if you stare, He will stay. And He will last.

Even if we won't.

CHAPTER 15

Hold On to Sixteen

Dear Children of Mine,

You've probably noticed that parents use a certain phrase over and over again. I know it's worn out, but sometimes it's the only thing left to say.

I'm guilty of it. In fact, if I don't say it out loud, I'm definitely *thinking* it, usually when I realize that you're doing something special for the first time—like driving, or going on a date, or when you ask me if I'll shut the door when you're down the basement with a member of the opposite sex (the answer is still no). Maybe I'm dropping you off at your first job, or I'm leaving you at a place that will become your new home for a while. Parents everywhere, just like me, will agree that as we walk away, it's on the tip of our tongues, because we don't know how it happened, and it hurts more than you'll ever know.

The phrases go a little something like this (or some variation): *I don't know where the time went*—or—*It goes by so fast*—or—*Don't blink, you might miss it.*

Mostly I ask myself, *Wasn't this kid just in diapers?*

And so, this letter is for you. Yes, all four of you. Not just for now, but for that special someday when you face the inexplicable wonder of learning that you're about to become a parent. I'm taking my stand, and in so doing, I hereby promise that I won't say it. I won't warn you about how fast it goes. In fact, if you're reading this and the day is drawing near to such an amazing and wondrous event, I'll bet you've already heard it a dozen times. By the time your son or daughter arrives, you'll have heard it a hundred times more.

Instead, let me explain to you *why* it goes by so fast in the first place.

Right now, time seems slower for you, or maybe just right, because it's all about, well . . . *you*. It's about your first experiences, crystallized in memories of living color. Your brain is soaking it all up in real time. Maybe it's that first crush or that first kiss. It could be your first job or that time you were in some serious trouble and didn't get caught, or you *did* get caught and you thought your life would end. Time stood still during that movie when you first held hands, when skin touched skin in an innocent sort of way. Perhaps it was a horrifying embarrassment at school—one that you'll dream about for the rest of your life. Maybe your heart stopped when you found out that you'd be saying goodbye to a friend who was moving away. Or to a four-legged friend, forever.

There are a lot of firsts, so just fill in the blank (I might not want to know about some of them).

In this span of time, from your early teenage years to that precise moment when you find out that another life is forming *because* of you, that's the truest form of time you'll ever know. It's the way it's supposed to feel. What happens before all of that is just a prologue to the raw edges of adolescence. You'll remember most of the single-digit years through old videos and pictures we force you to look at. But the middle school, high school, and immediate years that follow, whether in college or military or straight to a job—those are the years that will play like a movie in your head.

So please . . . make it a good one.

As to what happens after those years, I know I'm not alone in acknowledging that I have no idea where the last twenty-five years went. My time was here, just a minute ago, it would seem. I lost it and never found it again. I started what I thought was still my time with your mother and then it was split in two. Pretty soon it was more like a third to her two-thirds because weddings tend to set that stage. One child after another and twins in the middle, and with math being what it is, now I claim just a mere fraction of the time I used to call my own. Throw in moments where you caused me to lose my breath or you made my heart skip a beat, where my life flashed before my eyes because yours was in danger . . . then add in all of the sleep you made me lose along the way, well, it's no wonder it's gone in the blink of an eye.

It may seem a little cheesy, but as a wise Hoosier once said, "Hold on to sixteen as long as you can. Changes come around real soon, make us women and men."

So I promise. I won't say it. Just know that soon, your time will no longer be your own.

But you won't want it any other way.

Part Two

THE FIRST.
THE MARINE.

The one who would wrestle God if given the chance.

CHAPTER 16

You Took It Out

You wouldn't bend at the knees like other babies. I'd stand you up on my lap and you'd lock them. I'd push down on your little shoulders to get you to sit nicely, but it never worked. If you did give in, it was only so you could start jumping, and then you wouldn't stop, and you'd leave bruises on my thighs. It seems you've been jumping ever since.

You wouldn't snuggle into my chest. You'd push outward and challenge me with a feat of strength, crawl up onto my shoulder and look all around. I think you were trying to be at least as tall as me.

I remember being proud of you back then because when other babies' heads flopped all around and gazed cross-eyed at the world, you held your head straight and your neck firm and your eyes darted like lasers around the room. If a man walked by that you didn't know, you focused in on him and sized him up.

You sized me up a lot too, come to think of it. You were systematically analyzing me, testing for weak spots to exploit later. You focused those laser eyes on mine and soon they were arguing with me, even though you couldn't talk yet.

When you did decide to talk, there really wasn't a first word, because you just started speaking in full sentences. It was like you were waiting for the right moment to make your declaration. I clearly remember what you said:

"Mommy and Daddy are lying on the couch."

That's probably because we were exhausted.

Exhausted because you wouldn't take naps like other babies. You needed about five hours of sleep at night, maybe six if we were lucky, and you'd only *go* to sleep if the vacuum cleaner was running. Pretty soon I made a tape of the vacuum cleaner running. Then it seemed like one night we laid you down in your crib and at five in the morning, you were standing there in your crib, waiting for us. The next morning you stopped waiting and just crawled out.

I'm pretty sure we never potty trained you. I think you took off your own diaper and that was the end of that.

We had to take you in for testing before you could enter kindergarten. The teacher came out and said in her twenty-five years of education that she had never seen anything like you. She put you through to first grade because she thought you'd be bored in kindergarten. Maybe you were also bored in first grade, because that's when we got to know your teacher and the school principal very well.

You may not remember your first stunt, on your very first day of school, but I do.

You took it out.

That's right.

You. Took. It. Out.

Just like that famous *Seinfeld* episode. Maybe you thought it needed air, or maybe you wanted to show it off, but either way, that's when we got to know the school psychologist too.

A couple of weeks later, your teacher took something away from you. I don't remember what it was, but it was something very special to you and it was distracting you from paying attention in class. The teacher put it up very high where normal children would never dare attempt to retrieve it. A little while later your teacher stepped outside to talk with another teacher. In that moment, you took her dare and constructed a ladder out of chairs and desks and retrieved that something very special while the normal children cheered.

The first time I met your second-grade teacher, she had tears in her eyes. They weren't tears of joy. She suggested medication might help, and I wasn't sure if she meant for you or for the rest of us.

We knew lots of parents around this time who also had kids your age, and they were such well-behaved little boys and sweet little girls that we figured we were the worst parents ever. We tried taking a course called Growing Kids God's Way, but soon we learned we'd be stuck growing you your way.

You learned how to play the drums, and one time I watched you come and play for your little sister and brothers at their school. You sent me a perfectly spelled text with one hand in your pocket while you were still on stage drumming, and I don't think you missed a beat.

I still haven't figured that one out.

When you turned sixteen, you got a tattoo on your arm. It's a picture of a cross with the wind swirling around it or some such thing. We've taught you a lot about God over the years and about that cross, but I think if you met God in person you would wrestle Him and try to put Him a headlock. You'd tell Him you believe in Him but that you need to fight Him instead. Just like you do everything else.

Speaking of fighting, when I caught you smoking in the upstairs bathroom, you said you were just trying to light a Milk Duds box on fire. And you really thought I'd believe that? I argued that it didn't smell like that kind of smoke and why in the world would anyone want to light a Milk Duds box on fire anyway? But you presented your evidence and shouted your objections and conducted your cross-examination, and by the time your defense rested I almost believed you.

I don't think you were ever designed for the classroom and your grades reflected that. So you took a firefighting course your senior year and were the first one to volunteer to repel down a very tall building. Later on, your instructor, the city's fire chief, looked me straight in the eye and told me that he'd been around a long time and he'd had a lot of young men come through his program, and he didn't say this very often to too many parents, but he wanted me to know that I had a very special son.

And I believed him.

You had a bit of a hot temper when you were a teenager, and you punched some holes in our walls and stomped out of the house and you made your mother cry. But then you'd always come home and admit you were wrong and apologize and hug us and tell us how much you loved us. You had to lean down to hug us and we'd try to hang on to the wide span of your back and shoulders and pull you in tight because you never stood still, and you wouldn't stop jumping and moving and you wouldn't stop leaving with your friends.

You had a lot of friends, just like you do now, and that always made us smile.

You signed up to become a Marine on the 70th anniversary of the attack on Pearl Harbor. I'm pretty sure that made your grandparents proud, especially your grandfather who remembers the actual day Pearl Harbor was attacked. They pray for you all the time, just like we do because God knows we need all the help we can get.

You left for boot camp on September 11th. That made us all proud.

Shortly after you enlisted, before you left for San Diego, your recruiter told you that you scored so high on the military entrance exam that you qualified for pretty much every job they had.

I can't even begin to break down the irony of all of this, but I think it somehow started with a baby who wouldn't bend at the knees; the very one who would size up strangers with laser eyes; the little boy who made a ladder out of desks and chairs; the teenager who texted while drumming, lit that Milk Duds box on fire, and rappelled down a tall building.

The one who would probably wrestle God if given the chance.

Before you left, we heard that boot camp for the Marines was about breaking you down to nothing so that they could build you back up into who they wanted you to be. To that, your mother and I said, "Have at it," because that never worked for us.

While I won't ever forget that little boy you were, I'm proud of the man . . . the Marine . . . you're about to become.

CHAPTER 17

No News Isn't Very Good News

Your first letter home took way too long. We waited eighteen days, and when it finally showed up, it wasn't even a letter. It was a postage due notice because someone, namely you, neglected to put enough stamps on the envelope. This would be typical of you, of course, blindsiding me about the money I owe someone else for something you did.

But this time it didn't matter.

Your mother dropped everything and drove to that post office as fast as she could. When she got there and forked over the cash, she was handed a plastic bag and inside was your letter and another letter from your drill instructor and a brochure about your graduation. Apparently, you thought that the mail fairies would overlook you cramming as much as you could into a tiny envelope with one measly stamp (when it needed four) and that they'd gently fly it to us because it was literally ripping at the seams. I'm not sure we ever taught you about postage or mail service in general. It never came up as a topic of conversation, you know, because of the world we live in. Funny that it's 2012, yet here we are, caught in some time warp, watching the mailbox like a couple of kids waiting to get a letter from their buddy at summer camp.

Your mother writes you every day, as you know. She can't stand the thought of you facing a day without some type of mail from home. Not on her watch.

You see, it's been rough, navigating the waters of the absence you left behind, and waiting for some kind of sign—anything really—to let us know you've been all right these past few weeks. We know you're safe at boot camp. Of course, everything we hear and read is that no news is actually good news, especially early on. No news means you aren't hurt. No news means you haven't quit. No news means you're sticking with it and, with each passing day of no news, you're that much closer to becoming a Marine.

But it's still been excruciating, you know—the waiting.

You've been missed, though not always in the traditional way. There's the obvious stuff, like more food to eat and more drinks in the fridge. Also, we don't have your friends living in our basement anymore. Life has become neater, more orderly, and quiet, even with your three younger siblings still here. Honestly, it was as if you were too big for the house. Something deep inside of you was busting to get out and the rest of us were in the way. We weren't always getting along either, and so it felt like it was time. But now that you're gone and we've all started to color in between the lines again, maybe we're not so sure we want to color that way.

The last time your mother and I saw you, you hugged us tightly, and then kissed us both on the cheek, which you never do. You got on a bus with just the clothes on your back and a manila envelope with some paperwork and your airplane ticket. You had a Bible and your wallet too. You were flying all the way across the country to a place you'd never been, and into a world we'd never been.

You were a bit frantic because they had put you in charge of some of the other recruits. I wasn't quite sure what that meant, and you didn't have time to explain it, but I took it as a good sign.

You've always had that ever-important first impression on your side. You walk up to people, lean inward, shake hands like you mean it, and smile big and wide like it's the most natural thing to do.

I had to smile myself because when you got on that bus with your jeans too low and the top of your boxers too high, I had a feeling that was the last time I'd see that fashion statement. I walked to the car with the sensation of that strange kiss on my cheek, so proud of you, and more than a little bit scared for you.

Your mom cried all the way to the car, but I'm sure you knew that would happen.

We got the call from you in the middle of the night so that you could tell us that you had arrived safely in San Diego. You had to read from a script and you had about three seconds to spit it out while a drill instructor was screaming in your ear. We expected the call, and because your mother knew she'd have precious seconds, she didn't answer "hello." She just picked up the phone and said, "I love you." You responded that "Recruit Jacobson has arrived safely" because the moment you arrived, you were only allowed to speak in the third person (though I think you sneaked in an "I love you too").

It was an epic three seconds. I could hear the shouting coming through the phone's receiver, all the way on the other side of the bed. It was straight out of some movie we've all seen, and maybe wished we hadn't. It left me a little bit shaken because it wasn't a movie this time.

Either way, all that mattered was that we now had your letter. It was like gold in that little plastic bag. It was all of two pages, but you had touched the paper, and you had written down words on it. You assured us you were alive. You told us that you loved us, and you missed us and that you were going to make us proud. You had made it through the first week, and you were so happy because actual Marines told you that was the worst week. You told me specifically that when you get back, you'll beat me in arm wrestling, and I think you're a little delusional about that, maybe from lack of sleep, but whatever helps you get through these next three months is fine with me.

You started boot camp on September 11th, and you will graduate on December 7th. I think those are amazing days to start as a recruit and finish as a Marine.

Your letter was dated ten days earlier than the day we got it, because of the aforementioned postage issue. We've gone from eighteen years of near-constant communication to reading a letter today about how you were feeling ten days ago, at a time you probably need us the most, which is right about now. That's not going to happen, though, and I know it's all by design. You're being honed and shaped and sharpened into one of those men who fit a certain description—a description reserved only for a few, and the proud. It will forever define you, no matter what.

While I was writing this down, we got another letter. It also had postage due. It was a letter just for your mom, and you had taped three seashells that you'd found on the beach in San Diego. Your entire platoon was enduring some form of punishment in the sand that the rest of society will never understand, and yet you still hid away three shells because you knew they were your mom's favorites. Maybe there will always be a few soft edges on the inside of you that those drill instructors can't get at.

The pieces of paper you write on are now found here and there, all around our house, because your mother and I and your brothers and sister keep picking them up and reading and rereading them because it's all we have of you, at least for now.

Keep writing more, please, because it turns out that no news isn't very good news for us.

And by the way, if the envelope feels a little heavy, it's okay to splurge on the stamps.

CHAPTER 18

You're Not the Same Boy

We flew out to your graduation last week. When we arrived on base, we kept looking for you, even just a glimpse of you among all the others. They taunted us with your drills and exercises from afar as you marched with your fellow Marines. Thankfully, the platoon turned and you came a little closer. You must have seen us because you leaned back ever so slightly so that we could pick you out of the crowd.

I've never seen a dance or choreography quite like it. You were among eighty-six young men, but you were like a flock of birds, all moving and turning as one, as if somehow invisibly attached to each other. The intensity of shouting was deafening at times, and at others it would be a subtle, harmonized response of "Yes, Staff Sergeant," delivered with such a gentle deference that it gave me goose bumps.

Later, you were finally allowed to approach us, sharply adorned in your uniform. I noticed right away that you were skinny, and that your new posture was arrow straight. You neatly folded your hands behind your back while you carefully placed your feet apart at shoulder's length. Every motion you made was intentional and smooth as silk. My favorite motion was when you opened your arm to lead your mother around the base.

And it wasn't just your mother who received such treatment. Every female you came across was regarded with a nearly unnatural chivalry and the utmost respect. I tried to teach you this while you were growing up, but I'm not sure it stuck. Those drill instructors must have beaten it into your psyche. It was as if they trained you how to kill a man with your right hand while opening a door for your mother with your left.

Speaking of being trained to kill, suffice it to say, I won't be messing with you any longer.

Right after you were done with your graduation, we asked you what you wanted to do and where you wanted to go. All you wanted to do was sit down. Apparently, they hadn't let you sit for three months. I thought maybe you were joking, but then I realized you were deadly serious.

I cringed at some of the stories you shared from boot camp, and your mother looked as if she might cry. I knew they were going to break you down and build you back up into a Marine, but I never would have imagined such tactics. I won't even share them here, because you've earned the right to do so, not me. Either way, your brothers snickered as if justice had finally been served. Your little sister, however, looked on with admiration. She's been told a hundred times that no man would ever dare harm her with a big brother like you, but now it was starting to sink in.

When you became a Marine, you could speak in the first person again. Instantaneously you were treated like a human being, but I don't think it was a smooth transition for you. How could it be? Some of your drill instructors called you over so that you could introduce your family to them, and it looked as if your entire equilibrium was off because they were speaking to you and not shouting at you. I don't know if it was fear or relief I saw in your eyes. If it was both, fear was winning.

There's so much more to write, but let me just say, you're not the same boy I dropped off in September. There were a lot of proud fathers on your graduation day, but deep down inside you had to know which one was the proudest.

This probably won't be the end of the letters I write to you. Plenty more will need to be written about your service as a Marine. In fact, for those of us who've followed your trajectory since you were a little boy, we all know this is just the beginning.

CHAPTER 19

Gabriel, Blow Your Horn

You turn nineteen today, which is tomorrow for us because you're in Japan. I don't think we've ever been away from you on your birthday, but right about now you're as far away as you can be.

Seems to me that just a moment ago you were all squirmy and purple, gasping for your first breath of air. The doctor shouted, "Gabriel, blow your horn!" and soon after you let out a huge scream and our life has never been the same. I was supposed to be filming your arrival on the scene, but I lost all sense of time and space, so I stood in front of the camera on its tripod for most of it. We have a lot of footage, close-up, of a shirt I picked out to wear in July of 1994.

That squirmy little purple thing has now grown into you, a man who is very big with tattoos and muscles and rough hands; a man who still lives a huge scream of a life, hugs me and cracks the bones in my back to the point where I think I might break; a man who possesses a certain set of skills, the special kind that allows people to sleep peacefully at night, over here, away from it all.

You were made for this. Everyone who knows you believes you're in the right place, doing the right things. I'm not always sure of your motivations, but that's personal anyway. I know when Jimmy and many others died in those Towers, you were only seven, but you got so angry at the injustice of it all and by the sixth grade you had decided you wanted to be in the military. I remember how your soft brown eyes would become almost black as you grew older, nearly every time you would talk about it, because by then you had found friends just like Jimmy and you knew what it would be like to lose someone like him. In an instant. A lot of people reading this knew Jimmy too, and I think they'd be very happy to know, in some small way, that you've got his back.

If that was the only reason you joined, it would seem reason enough.

Happy birthday, Private First Class Jacobson, USMC

CHAPTER 20

You're My Badge of Honor

A few days ago, I was at a party and saw a man who was in great shape with big muscular arms and tattoos and he looked like the military type. I introduced myself and he confirmed that he'd been in the service for six years as military police. I told him a little about you, of course, with pride, because I do that a lot these days. I speak of you like I know what I'm talking about, like you're my badge of honor, as if I should somehow be a recipient of the same kind of respect you deserve. This is silly, of course, but I did change your diapers and I did teach you a thing or two. And I did survive eighteen years of you living under my roof. So, yes, I will claim a partial stake in the who and the what you've become.

Anyhow, the point of all of this is that a little bit later this very muscular man was demonstrating for us some type of martial arts for which he'd been trained for weeks or maybe months, and suffice it to say, whatever he was doing looked very Jason Bourne-ish and I suspect the person on the receiving end of it would be in a lot of pain. I was in awe just watching it.

Now, while I hold this man in the highest regard for his service to our country, you should know that the particular military branch in which he served was not yours. And because of that, on your birthday, I wanted to share with you the rest of the story.

As I said, he was showing us these moves and they were pretty impressive. I chimed in, while elbows and arms were flying, making small talk, and said something to the effect of, "I wonder if they taught my son how to fight like that?"

It was an innocent question because I honestly didn't know. I know how you can handle yourself in new and efficient ways because when you come for a visit I'll challenge you to a brawl and you'll take my hand and twist it a certain way so that I drop to my knees in a matter of seconds. I know your friends sometimes jump you for sport and probably wish they hadn't. But I still don't know all that you're fully capable of, and maybe I don't want to know. Either way, I was just trying to weave you back into the conversation, because, as a proud father, I'm pretty much in awe of what you do too.

His response wasn't what I expected: "Oh, it wouldn't matter if they taught him how to fight like this or not. I would never mess with a Marine."

There was no pause. It came out just like that. He had never seen you before, yet here was this big intimidating guy in front of me, and for all he knew you could have been some pipsqueak or skinny punk that he could squash like a bug, but he didn't hesitate for a moment to talk about you—what you had to endure for weeks on end and the intense training you're constantly under and the brotherhood you enjoy that makes you, as a Marine, so very special. I knew this, of course, but it was nice to hear all over again. I suspect there's a lot of competition between the branches of military service—a lot of bravado and a lot of talk—but this guy took the attention off himself and paid you some serious respect.

I was glad I had my sunglasses on because something about that moment made me catch my breath a little and, well, that's all you need to know about that.

Right about now you're on a ship somewhere in the Pacific, undergoing even more training, so getting a birthday gift to you today would be for naught, but I still hope this story makes you smile on your special day. We're all so proud of you and love you very much.

Happy 20th Birthday, Lance Corporal Jacobson, USMC

P.S. Later I beat that very muscular military man in an arm wrestle, which I'm sure will make your birthday even happier. Your old man still has a few tricks left.

Come to think of it, maybe he let me win because he didn't want to mess with a Marine's father either.

CHAPTER 21

Don't Blow Snot Rockets

Well, young man, here's a list of twenty-one suggestions for your twenty-first birthday. Now I realize you're in the Marines and you're pretty smart, but it's still good to have something in writing from your old man, you know . . . just in case I get hit by a bus or something.

1. Love God and love people. It really is that simple.

2. Don't upset your mother. Almost as important as #1.

3. In fact, don't upset your father either. And while I'm at it, don't upset your grandparents. Take good care of us because there's a blessing promised if you do. It's in the Bible.

4. Give money to those people who are holding signs at traffic lights, or the ones who approach you on the street. It might be a scam, but for a few bucks here or there, you can afford to overlook it.

5. Proper grammar when writing (or speaking) is very important. It delivers a telegram of competence. Of course, this doesn't give

you the right to correct the mistakes of others. That delivers a different kind of telegram.

6. All the ant traps in the package need to be used at once. They work together in some mysterious way.

7. Listerine (or its cheaper store-brand equivalent) works just as well as flossing.

8. When you run out of dishwasher detergent, dish soap—in said dishwasher—is not a good replacement. Trust me, I know.

9. Try Rain X before you replace your windshield wipers.

10. Turn on the exhaust fan when you take a shower. Moisture trapped in a small room isn't good.

11. Don't be the guy who waits until the last minute when traffic is merging. Be the guy who lets in the guy who waits until the last minute when traffic is merging.

12. Don't use body wash. It's a scam. Plus, well, you're a guy.

13. Tithe. Always. Ten percent off the gross and then some. Start young and increase the percentage as you are able.

14. Take a baby aspirin every day. If the medical community agrees on one thing, this may be it.

15. Stinginess is not an attractive quality. When you're out with friends for dinner, don't be nitpicky about the bill.

16. Speaking of that dinner, always, always be nice to your waiter or waitress. Not just because he or she is serving you, but also

because it speaks volumes about the type of person you are, especially to the people you're dining with. Don't forget to tip generously.

17. Chivalry never goes out of style. Open the door for her. Pick up the bill. Respect her parents. Stop blowing snot rockets.

18. Reset the red button on your electrical outlets before you call an electrician. Also, press that button on the bottom of the garbage disposal before you call a plumber. That's two for the price of one.

19. Always respect and honor the Jewish people in your life and Israel as a nation. They are God's chosen—at the beginning, in the middle, and, most importantly, at the end of the story.

20. Follow Jesus. If religion or other Christians or maybe even church gets in the way of that, don't blame Jesus. It's not His fault. Follow Him and only Him and everything else will fall into place.

21. See #1.

Happy birthday, Sergeant Jacobson, USMC. I am very proud to be your father and so grateful for your twenty-one years on this planet. I'll try to come up with more suggestions for when you turn twenty-five, if I'm still around, which I probably will be (because of #14).

CHAPTER 22

A Certain Set of Acronyms

I sat down, held out my arm, and you were placed in it. The back of your head was in my open hand and the length of your body fit nicely, all the way to my elbow. You fell asleep there, and I balanced you for a while and inhaled the moment, locking away the memory that I might retrieve it someday.

I'm glad I did, because it never happened again. You woke up, wriggled your way out of my grasp, and, from that moment on, it seems you determined that such a ridiculous display of inactivity was completely out of the question.

You started to grow. And grow some more. Pretty soon we stopped measuring to see if you were taller than me and I admitted defeat. Still, I reminded you in subtle and not-so-subtle ways how a father holds sway over his son for a lifetime, because not so long ago I balanced the weight of you with one arm. And I reminded you of who it was that changed your diapers.

At your most helpless, you looked *to me*.

Through the years, you tried to tell us that you didn't fit in a classroom. You were that proverbial square peg, and we were forcing you into a round hole. We knew you were crazy smart, but you didn't apply it. Instead, you made *us* crazy because you applied yourself to finding trouble (which you were pretty good at, by the way). You skated by, content with merely passing in those classrooms.

Barely.

You were known for a certain set of acronyms, you know the kind, that parents like us tried to medicate, which was more like trying to lasso a bull and pull him out of a china shop without something breaking, knowing that one or two pieces would, but hoping they were the least expensive, the least precious.

Time went on, as did the growing, and soon that baby boy I held was not only a man, but a certain kind of man.

You've been gone for a while now, and you've proven everyone right. And by everyone, I mean the very people who stopped us and encouraged us with their caring, knowing expressions, looking into our tired eyes, telling us you'd be someone special someday. We smiled and nodded and hoped for the best.

You were right too. I was secretly hoping I could wait much longer to admit that, but I can't. You've probably learned more than you did in all those classrooms combined. Maybe even more than some do in a lifetime.

Now you live by some different acronyms. You've endured arguably the toughest boot camp on the face of the earth, at MCRD (Marine Corps Recruit Depot) in San Diego, followed by Marine Combat Training (MCT). Then you graduated from 29 Palms as a Field Radio Operator (FRO). You're a certified Combat Life Saver (CLS) and a licensed Humvee operator. You've earned a perfect Physical Fitness Test (PFT) and you're a part of a Firepower Control Team (FCT 5) within a Supporting Arms Liaison Team (SALT Charlie) at a unit called 5th ANGLICO, you're about to start ABC, which is ANGLICO Basic Course, securing your position with an elite fighting force. You were named the Iron Man and you just finished a grueling three-week course to become a Marine Combat Instructor of Water Survival (MCIWS), a title held by only 1 percent of those in the Marine Corps. Barely a month goes by without you calmly telling us about another honor or a credential or an acronym you've received.

You're a Marine now. A highly trained machine. With wars and rumors of wars, it gets a little dicey being your father. In fact, much like eighty years ago, we're seeing another advance of pure evil. I don't think anyone wants to admit it because we think we've come so far—we're so chic and sophisticated compared to those grainy black-and-white images. But the truth is, history repeats itself. This new threat is spreading like a cancer without a cure anywhere in sight.

And just like back then, it's one of biblical proportions.

I lean in a little more to the news, ever attentive, and I wait. And I worry. Right about now I wish you were made for those classrooms, but I know that you've found your square hole and now you fit. Simply put, our threats of retribution can't be made against such evil without the collective will and strength of men and women like you, Gabe. You are the promise that hides behind the words of our leaders who only find sense and clarity and resolve when they mention the very likes of you and what it is you will deliver.

I really don't want you to be the one who must go and fight them. But I know you very well, from the moment you wriggled out of my grasp. A ridiculous display of inactivity as our response is completely out of the question. You've been through some of the toughest training on the planet, and you're ready. If even a fraction of those serving alongside you possess your same strength and ability, there's no human force on earth we can't defeat.

At our most helpless, we will look *to you*.

CHAPTER 23

Dear Future Wife of Gabe

Dear Future Wife of Gabe,

I'm having trouble picturing you and sometimes wonder if you even exist. I hope you do because you've been prayed for—a lot—so you hold a special place in the hearts of everyone who knows and loves your future husband.

The truth is, I like writing about Gabe, so this is a good excuse for me to do so. Not only is he my firstborn son, but he's the type of muse that every writer dreams about—one who has provided an unending supply of material and inspiration during his nearly twenty-three years on this planet. I don't completely understand him, so in some strange way I get to know him better by writing about him.

Over the years, Gabe has ushered in a wide variety of emotions to our home: the highs, the lows, and the in-betweens, heightened at times to a near frenzy that I still can't explain. Sometimes his mother and I wonder if we raised him or just did our best to contain him. Being with Gabe, knowing him, loving him, well—the closest I can explain to unsuspecting others is that it's like wading into the ocean when there's a wave off in the distance. Not just any wave, mind you, but one of those gigantic ones, like in Hawaii—the kind the surfers hope for with the tubes and the breaks.

There you'll be in the shallow water on the shore, up to your ankles and then your knees, and you'll see him rising on the horizon, and as he rushes toward you, you'll get sucked in; the undertow will have you, but that's okay because you'll want to experience him—*everything* about him draws you in—his body language, his smile, his energy.

His mother and I dove into that ocean. We had surfboards once, just like the one you'll need. We had the skill set and the strength, maybe even some energy, so we were able to anticipate him; we could hop on our boards at just the perfect moment, ride it out, and love him and the adventure of it all. Sometimes it was great and exhilarating. Other times, that wave came crashing down around us. Our timing would be all wrong and we'd get shot out of the tube too late, thrown off our boards, tumbling, disoriented, and not exactly sure which way we were facing as we came up for air.

Now we just watch and float nearby, still experiencing that wave but out on the fringes and the easy side. We're just near enough that we feel the undulation of him and the life he leads. We appreciate and respect that wave's enormity and power, danger even. Daring ones still take the chance and know the thrill as he carries them to the shore. That wave—your future husband—can be awe-inspiring and brilliant. Even now, after the wave is gone, we always want it to come back, just as much as we need the ocean to calm in between. We need some time to talk about what just happened.

Gabe just happened. He is a life force.

If none of that makes sense, here's something else: I think you'll have to be chill, as the kids say; maybe a little like me—one part pleaser, two parts easygoing, and three parts strong enough to stand your ground when needed. Don't worry about being too laid back because Gabe will sharpen any dull edges you might have. He'll handle the extremes and the excesses of any emotion you might be under-indulging within your cozy, rational boundaries. If you're mad about something, expect him to become enraged on your behalf. If you're sad, he'll double down and find you there, go deeper than your sadness and push you up from beneath, maybe from some dark place he's already occupying. If you're excited or happy and you need him to match it, count on him to multiply it and take you to an altogether better place called euphoria. He still jumps around like a little kid when he's excited about something. Literally.

You'll figure out soon, if you don't know it already, that Gabe has more friends than any of us can count. There's a reason for that. I imagine you're in for a lifetime of those friends and his brothers from the Marines pulling you aside to share a story or two with big smiles on their collective faces. Some of those stories you might not want to hear.

Your future husband is incredibly loyal to his friends and family. Let him be, and rest in that loyalty. It comes as naturally to him as anything. He was five when his twin brothers were born, and he's taken his responsibility for them very seriously. I've wished at times that his influence on them would have been more, uh . . . *constructive*, but then again, brothers have a special bond and I've never once doubted his devotion to them. He would protect them with his life.

And don't get me started on his little sister, the one who arrived on the scene a couple years later. I shudder at the thought of anyone harming her—obviously because of the harm to her— but nearly as much for what might happen to the person foolish enough to attempt such a thing. I've seen his eyes darken when he speaks of this and I don't even know him anymore. You will have that same protection. That devotion. That loyalty. Your children will someday know it. He will be their hero and the best bodyguard ever.

This kid of mine, a grown man for sure, will always be my little boy. He is a gift beyond measure to so many, yet he doesn't even know it most of the time, so you'll need to affirm him. Don't allow him to forget that he was so smart he skipped over kindergarten, but so much trouble that he nearly didn't graduate high school. Help him navigate who he is. I don't always speak his language, but I have a feeling you'll be fluent in it. Remind him that he was barely twenty-one when he became a sergeant in the Marines, with more accolades than most of us know for a lifetime, but he still doesn't tap into his full potential, nor scratch the surface of what he can accomplish. Maybe before long, you'll be nodding in agreement. He is a paradox in that regard, knowing that he could do anything he wanted but hesitant to harness the power of his wave and the wake of it, the undertow with which he draws us all in.

Lastly, when Gabe was leaving for boot camp a while back, I wrote that we had taught him a lot about God over the years, but if he met Him in person he'd try to wrestle Him and put Him a headlock. Gabe believes in God, but he'd rather fight Him instead. I pray you'll help him realize there's no need to fight his Creator. It's okay to submit to someone, and God is the perfect choice for that.

It's safe to say that I'm forever a changed person because of the man you'll be marrying. I know a lot of fathers say such things of their kids, but your future husband has had a profound impact on my life. I'm simply a better man for having had him as my son.

Even when the ocean calms, I still want that wave to come back.

Part Three

THE TWINS

With the second child,
you'll notice how his whole face smiles,
not just his mouth, and how that makes you smile too.

With the third, well, he's fearless in a way
that I don't understand.

CHAPTER 24

A Goodbye to Bikinis

After you two came into the world, I would often get asked if twins ran in our family. I never checked, because twins seemed to run in the family of a certain infertility drug I was injecting into your mom's leg. So, with no real answer, and after all she had to go through to get pregnant, I figured we earned the right to say, "They do now."

Be that as it may, the two of you burst onto the scene sixteen years ago today. Back then, the hospital still allowed twins to be born in those colorful birthing rooms with cable TV and recliners and bad art on the walls. Little did anyone know that such a policy would end abruptly because the Jacobson twins scared the bejeezus out of some doctors and nurses and, in no short measure, me. Legend has it that, the very next day, all multiple births had to take place in a surgical room.

The morning started out like it was supposed to, and the young doctor arrived just like she was supposed to, but you two didn't arrive at all like you were supposed to. Tate, you decided you'd come out the normal way, but you took forever and by the time you did emerge, you were this sick blue-gray color like a Monday-morning sky in February. It could be that your twin brother was choking you or something worse that brothers do to each other when no one is looking. I didn't get to see your face because the nurses rushed you out of the room. You weren't breathing on your own, and that's never a good thing.

A few seconds later, a holy panic registered on that young doctor's face, because you, Levi, must have liked all the extra room in there, so you decided you weren't going to come out at all. Your mother was already exhausted by Tate and the epidural that didn't take. Then there was some hushed talk of "breach" and some quick glances between medical professionals, and I wondered what they were keeping from me. Suddenly, the doctor said she had to call in a specialist. I thought all OB-GYNs were specialists, you know, at delivering babies, but there was a multiple-birth-high-risk-pregnancy specialist doctor who just so happened to be on another floor of the hospital.

And he was needed in a mighty big hurry.

After about a minute of awkward silence, that specialist ran into the room like he had sprinted across county lines, and pretty soon I understood why they were using hushed tones. He literally pushed the non-specialist out of the way and I remember feeling bad for her. All at once he was wheeling your mom out of the room and down a long hall to surgery with her legs up in the air. There was a lot of yelling and commotion right about then, and some regular people in that hall who were waiting for normal babies to arrive got a quick glance at your mom's bits and pieces.

A nice nurse led me to a window right outside that surgical room. It was about the size of a TV screen, like I was about to watch a show or something. It turned out to be a horror show. I still remember the feel of the chair against the back of my knees, the very chair she pushed up against me because she said that the amount of blood I was about to see was going to affect me in ways that I didn't have the capacity to appreciate. It might be better, she said, if I sat down before I fainted and fell down instead.

I decided to stand, and I watched as they started cutting into your mom and it was awful. Something strange happens when someone you love is being hurt and you are a witness to it. Maybe it's just me, but I feel it in my bones, like when a music teacher hits a tuning fork on a table to find perfect pitch. I felt it just like that. My bones were vibrating with a perfect pitch of pain, and all I could do was stand there.

Anyhow, it's important to note that planned C-section deliveries are precise and sanitary and by the book, but emergency C-sections are anything but. Your mom was screaming at the real doctor that she could feel him cutting her open because of that epidural not working, but there wasn't any time to fix that, so he put a mask on her face and put her under completely and then tore into her abdomen as her arms hung lifeless to her side. They reached in to grab you, Levi, but you were lifeless too. You weren't even a shade of blue or gray like your brother. You were a dark greenish color and you were dead.

I remember the doctor holding you and how your little body unfolded in his hands. For all I knew, at that very moment your twin brother was with you once again, but in an altogether better place. Your mother didn't look so great either; I've never seen so much blood. It was everywhere. While they were working on you, she laid there, unnaturally pale with this huge cavity exposed. I didn't know which way to turn so I finally sat down in that chair they brought for me and I prayed. For about a minute or two, I prayed the prayer of a desperate man who is about to lose nearly everything.

In just one morning.

As some stories go, this one took a much better turn, and, of course, it had a very happy ending. I stood up after praying, and those doctors and nurses revived you, Levi, and brought you back to life right before my very eyes. That horror show in the window became one of joy and hope and blessing.

After things calmed down a bit, I was allowed to see you and your brother, who was also given plenty of special attention that day. There you were, right next to each other, connected to all sorts of wires, but at least now you were the best shade of pink and peach I had ever seen. Your mother rested quietly in the adjacent room, sleeping off the anesthesia. Thanks to your collective stubbornness, it would be a long and painful recovery for her (with a goodbye to bikinis for a lifetime) but seeing your sweet faces and holding you both in her arms made it all worth it.

We picked your names just because we liked them, but we found out later what they meant. Tate, your name means cheerful. For those of us who know and love you, I'm not sure there could ever be a more perfect name. You have the uncanny ability to be able to walk into a room and, with very little effort, lift spirits and make people smile. It is a true gift, just as you are to us.

Levi, your name means attached or pledged. And joined, which we're so glad you eventually decided to do, albeit in such a way that changed hospital policy. You were also named after one of Jacob's sons, which is quite fitting given your last name. You have such a calming effect on us, with your understated confidence, your wry sense of humor, and your easy blue eyes.

Despite your dramatic entries, and without much fuss or fanfare, you've grown into two boys who make us so proud. You both seem to take everything in stride as if conquering a day like that right out of the gate prepared you well for whatever life might throw your way.

If anyone ever asks if twins run in our family, for all you two had to go through to get here, you've more than earned the right to say . . .

"We do now."

CHAPTER 25

The Ugly Store

The near-constant fighting, both verbal and physical, between twin brothers is entertaining at times and exhausting at others. It's like jungle warfare between these two. One must always be vigilant for a sneak attack from the other, and a premeditated retaliation is usually desirable. To get caught with one's shorts down is simply unacceptable and, quite literally, one of them usually ends up this way.

I'm not sure how old they were when the insults started flying, but I remember driving them somewhere and Levi leaned over in his car seat and said, "Hey, Tate, the ugly store just called, and they want your face back."

Tate's retort was a little slow in coming, due to inexperience, but still not bad for his age; it was something to the effect of, "Yeah, that's because they sold out of yours."

Not too long afterward, we were getting ready to leave on a vacation and I was yelling at the kids to collect the garbage. Gabe, our oldest, replied that he'd get the upstairs, and Chloe, our youngest, said that she'd get the trash in the basement. Tate replied, without missing a beat, "I'll get Levi."

If it's not spoken, there's always some form of bodily attack that's either imminent or in process when they're near each other. A shove, a last-minute well-placed foot, a martial arts-style Muay Thai body kick—whatever one can think of to send the other sprawling across the floor (extra points are scored if this takes place in stores or other people's homes with nice things). Their older brother would encourage it for his own entertainment, so it's a wonder that I haven't seen one of them come through a wall yet, like a stuntman on a movie set. God forbid they sit next to each other on a couch to watch a movie, and you can be assured that if there's an event where we sit together as a family, all in a row, there's a plan in place to keep them at opposite ends of our seating arrangement.

Despite their incessant need to physically abuse, if they should end up next to each other at the dinner table and it's time to hold hands and pray, they'll only put their hands somewhere in the vicinity of each other. To actually touch in this way would be much too intimate. Indeed, their skin is only meant to come in contact when a fist hits an arm and leaves a bruise, or an open hand hits a naked back, creating the dreaded five-star. The only hugging they do of any consequence is when Tate wrestles Levi to the ground so he can fart in his face. I'll spare you my recounting of some of the other things they do to each other, like the one that has something to do with a goat, as in the verb, not the noun.

They're not identical twins, and they've never worn the same clothes. There's no secret language between them unless you count arguing. Who knows, maybe it started at birth when Tate was born the usual way and Levi disagreed with that route, so he came out via C-section. On top of that, their personalities are as opposite as night and day, and one is much larger than the other. One is a rule enforcer and the other is a rule bender. One eats healthy foods, the other not so much. On school nights, one must be forced to go to sleep and the other is asleep by nine.

Thankfully, they have friends who consider them a package deal. I've heard too many stories of one twin left out while the other successfully navigates life's social circles. They do tend to stick together, and maybe even watch each other's backs, at least long enough to plan a sneak attack (see the shorts-down reference above).

I suppose the main reason I write this is to remind myself and parents of young brothers (who may not know what's coming) that despite these incessant attacks on each other, there really is something mysterious, ever loyal and true, and maybe even love (yikes), that takes place between brothers, should someone else choose to attack.

It just so happens that both boys play lacrosse, which, if you didn't know, can be a brutal sport, almost as bad as football. Lacrosse puts the term "contact sport" into proper perspective. While you're not supposed to tackle opposing players, you do get to hit them with a stick, and if you happen to knock them to the ground (legally, of course), all the better.

A few years ago, Levi, the smaller of the twins, was playing at one end of the field, and he took a hit from three opposing players who were running in a pack. It flattened him. Literally. It was quick and dirty and looked painful. He never saw it coming.

But, from the other end of the field, someone else did.

The collective hit from these punks bordered on illegal, but they got away with it and ran off with the ball. As they approached our goal, they encountered some limited resistance from another player on our team, who somehow managed to knock the ball free. While everyone stopped momentarily, grasping for the ball, that "someone else" saw his chance. Tate leveled his stick from about twenty feet away, and everyone knew what was coming. He ran at them like a crazed bull and clothes-lined all three of them. They fell to the ground like tin soldiers, all in a row. The refs threw their yellow flags and the piercing sounds of their whistles filled the air like fireworks. Tate ran off the field, and I caught a smile on his face as he made his way to the penalty box.

I'm sure that before we even got home from that game, Tate

and Levi argued in the van about this or that, insults flying about spots available on the girl's team or using a peanut shell for an athletic cup, and nary a word was uttered about the revenge hit of the century.

That sort of interaction may be their comfort zone for a lifetime. I suppose that's okay with me, so long as their bond as brothers remains intact.

CHAPTER 26

Dear Future Wife of Tate

Dear Future Wife of Tate,

I'm looking forward to meeting you. I suppose right about now you're enjoying high school, two counties over or three or four states away, or maybe twenty. You might be looking forward to college or, who knows, possibly something else on the horizon.

To be honest, I think about you a lot. I pray for you too. You'll have to be an answer to prayer because no parent is able to guess these things. We hope and we wonder, but honestly, we have no idea. I suppose instead of knowing the type of woman you are, I have a better idea of the woman you'll become after marrying Tate. I'll get to that in a minute.

Here's the thing: Someday soon you'll find yourself in the company of a gentle giant. You'll hear his infectious laugh from around a corner, or maybe you'll see him as he's walking toward you from a distance. It could be that he'll sit next to you at a movie, or in class, or in a car. Once you're introduced, you'll be struck by his ash blue eyes, his easy manner, and his kindness. You'll notice how his whole face smiles, not just his mouth, and how that makes you smile too. Without knowing it, right about then, you will start to fall in love with my son.

You should know that Tate had a bit of a precarious start when he came into this world. He had trouble breathing, so by the time he was delivered his skin was the same color as his eyes. His twin brother was probably choking him in there, as brothers sometimes do. As a result, Tate spent a couple days in the intensive care unit, hooked up to wires and tubes and such, and he looked just like Karl Malden. You're too young to know who that is, so Google him when you get a chance. Thankfully, before too long, he left that hospital behind, grew into his nose, and became a cute little guy.

Once home, it became clear Tate was going to be a unique and quirky sort of baby. He liked to fall asleep on the kitchen countertop near the stove with its fan set on high and a blanket wrapped around his head like a swami. As he grew a bit older and learned to talk, he chose not to say much, content rather to let his smaller, more talkative twin brother handle the day-to-day communications. Tate seemed more like his bodyguard. To this day, I think he would do anything to protect his little brother.

And now, you.

Something else that's unique about Tate is that he's a back sleeper, which I assume you'll find out sooner or later. Yes, he eventually outgrew the countertop and his swami blanket, and now if you wake him up in the morning, you'll find him lying peacefully on his back, always the same way, like he's died and gone to heaven. They say that people who sleep this way are the strong silent types who don't like a big fuss; they're very loyal and love hearing the problems of others and will go out of their way to help. This is very true of Tate. He sleeps the way he lives, with a face that is pure calm. Pretty soon, you'll get to see that face every morning and know what it means to have someone like that by your side.

Now, of course, Tate has his faults, just like we all do, but as his father I struggle to describe them because he somehow makes those faults humorous and endearing. Despite the outward calm, he's easily distracted and tends to bounce all over the place. He can be impulsive and wants to know what's next instead of enjoying what's *now*. When he was little, he would ask about dinner before finishing his breakfast. I suppose the best way to put it is that you'll need to have an unwavering side to you. His opinions can be erratic and change mid-sentence, which might be funny now, but someday he'll need you to help him draw a line.

Tate also happens to be a scary driver, so please wear your seat belt. Before he was old enough to have his license, he nearly killed me on a go-cart ride. I was his passenger and the last thing I saw before crashing into a barn and certain death was his devious grin, as if he had planned all along to save me at the last minute. I've tried to avoid being his passenger now that he's driving a real car. Impulsiveness is not a good trait behind the wheel.

Getting back to the good stuff, while Tate doesn't sit still for very long, you'll find in his comings and goings that he's very perceptive to when someone isn't quite right, maybe a little off, or a little sad or angry. He reads people very well, especially his mother, and let me just say, for a man to be perceptive to anyone's feelings is special, but to have intuition like that for the opposite sex is a blessing. You'll come to appreciate that.

Tate has a lot of friends and people seem to genuinely enjoy his company. I think we've all benefited in some way because we're associated with him. Just the other day, a woman came up to our table at a restaurant to tell us what a good friend Tate has been to her daughter. I love hearing that, and while I'm humbled that he's my kid, you should know about it too because it speaks to his character.

While I've described his gentle way, Tate is a strong kid and he'll defend himself without giving it a second thought. He got suspended in middle school because he beat up a kid who jumped him from behind. I think his older brother, the Marine, taught him some moves he'll never forget. Tate also plays lacrosse and has a reputation for knocking people over just because he can, so he spends a lot of quality time in the penalty box. But just as soon as he would do that, he'd be the first to knock over sour moods with his quick smile and his near-constant effort to make sure everyone is okay. Tate is like an equilibrium manager for everyone's dispositions.

You won't have to be a great cook, but you might want to know some of his favorites. If you can handle those, you'll be just fine. If you can't cook at all, don't worry about it; he's a pretty good one himself. He's been thinking about what to make since breakfast.

So, when I mentioned earlier that I have a better idea of the woman you'll become after marrying Tate, I think you'll become a fortunate woman. I think you'll become a protected woman. I think you'll become a woman who knows what it's like to have a true friend and partner for life. You're also going to become a sister and a daughter and will inherit a big family that loves your husband very much, and now you too.

It may just be my perspective, but I think most young women are secretly hoping to find kindness in the man they'll someday marry. That's probably not on your radar right now. You think it will be good looks, or chemistry, or maybe a sense of humor, but trust me, kindness wins.

And now you win because you'll become the wife of Tate.

CHAPTER 27

Even More of a Beater

Sometimes I wonder if my children live their lives in such a way to create stories for me, or if I'm just the only one dumb enough to share them.

To begin, you should know that both boys hold down jobs at a local restaurant. This is important because at some weak moment, I agreed to buy them a car if they would help pay for it. Not a brand-new car, mind you, but more of a beater to get around. I figured I'd get them an old SUV or a truck, something that would keep them safe because of the inevitable crash into this or that. Plus, they drive their sweet little sister to and from school, so it couldn't be too much of a beater. We'll call it a pseudo-beater.

So, with the help of my car-savvy brother-in-law, I bought an old Acura MDX off Craigslist from some guy down in Florida. It had high mileage with the bonus of each of its four tires advertising a different brand and displaying varying degrees of baldness. The boys didn't really care. Aside from the engine running, they mostly wanted to know if it had a place to plug in an aux cord or a USB charging port for their phones. It had neither, so it's *that* kind of old.

Anyhow, it was set to be delivered on a Sunday afternoon, but out of the blue I got a call on a Saturday morning that it would be arriving early, as in, they'd-be-here-in-ten-minutes sort of early.

So I pulled myself together and met the delivery men in my church parking lot because I didn't think a semi could navigate down my street. The whole thing felt very suspicious, and between you and me, I think those delivery men may have been part of the Russian mob. (If you're in leadership at my church, I apologize for inviting the Russian mob onto church property. Oh, and if you're reading this and you happen to be a member of the Russian mob, those men did a very nice job delivering my pseudo-beater.)

Once the deal was done and the cash exchanged, I drove real stealth-like onto some side streets and took the back way to my house because my new purchase had no plates. It made a lot of noise going over bumps, but I turned up the music real loud which blared out of the one speaker that worked and, well, problem solved. The inside smelled of incense from some far-away, mystical land, and I didn't have to pay extra for that.

Now, while a separate story could be shared here about the Russian mob and the acquiring of my teenagers' exotic-smelling pseudo-beater, I'm writing this to share conclusive evidence in support of the many reasons why we choose beaters for teenagers in the first place.

The time had come for the boys to get their driver's licenses, in late January, on pretty much the only day this past winter when the roads were snow covered. We may have fudged a bit on how much practice time they had logged prior to that day, simply because the practice time had to be fifty hours (each) with a licensed driver over the age of twenty-five, preferably a family member, and while I tried really hard to be that family member, it became impossible for me to be a passenger for even five minutes with those boys driving, let alone the one hundred hours needed.

And this is because they scare the bejeezus out of me.

I happen to be a very defensive driver. I assume that everyone else on the road is either drunk or distracted (or both) and they're always on the verge of swerving into my lane or pulling in front of me or any number of things that drunk or distracted drivers do. Tate and Levi, on the other hand, drive as if every other driver on the road woke up that day with the sole purpose of clearing a path for them and getting out of their way.

With that said, we arrived at the Bureau of Motor Vehicles for that glorious rite of passage, and while the three of us were waiting for the instructor to come out, Levi asked me if I thought he and Tate would pass. I told him no, probably not, because they didn't practice enough with their mother. Levi smirked and thanked me for the confidence boost. (I really did think they would pass; I only said that, so they'd try harder to prove me wrong.)

Thankfully, they did indeed pass, and they got their brand-new licenses. I imagine it was based more on charm than actual driving ability, but that's beside the point. The instructor pulled me aside to tell me that Tate turned too wide and Levi turned too quickly, which I figured were easy things to fix, at least over time and more practice with their mother.

On the way home, as we were turning into our neighborhood, I reiterated what the instructor had just said. Of course, they wanted to leave immediately in their pseudo-beater and taste their new-found freedom, and it was announced that Tate would drive first. So I specifically told him, per the instructor, to watch his wide turns. I added for good measure that if he should be in a wreck on his first adventure, God forbid, that he should never, ever leave the scene of the accident. I reluctantly agreed to let them go, even though some unplowed snow and ice were on our neighborhood's streets. I went back to work, said a quick prayer, or a hundred quick prayers, and hoped for the best.

By the time I returned home later that evening, I noticed that at the front of our neighborhood a row of mailboxes had been hit. Not just grazed, mind you. There, with no one else around, it was like a bomb had gone off, with splintered wood from the base and pieces of mail and busted-up mailboxes littering the snow on the ground. I found this quite amusing given the lecture I had previously given Tate, and I felt bad for some poor soul who couldn't control his vehicle. I chuckled to myself as I observed a clear path in the icy sludge where the driver took a very wide turn, lost control, and hit the mailboxes, and then another clear path that led back onto the road by the very same driver who then left the scene of the accident.

I'm trying to think of a witty ending, but I don't have one, but let's just say there's a pseudo-beater which, before leaving the neighborhood, became even more of a beater. Consider it exhibit A of the aforementioned evidence as to why we buy beaters for teenagers.

And I'll let you draw your own conclusions as to who paid for a row of new mailboxes with the money he makes at a local restaurant.

P.S. I know, I know. I should have spent more time practicing with them.

CHAPTER 28

It's You People

I don't cry much.

I mean, I've had a few close calls over the years, usually when my daughter is dancing on stage, but I've managed to compose myself.

So, as you can imagine, whatever cry muscles exist in my face, around my eyes, in my jaw or my brain, or wherever cry muscles typically are, mine are out of shape and probably have been since about the age of six.

I'm sharing this now because over the last few weeks, I've been on the verge of—and even succumbed to—actual *crying*. Not the well-up-with-tears kind. I mean the *break-down-and-wail* kind.

My wife and daughter are pros at crying. They do it gracefully, like a work of art. They expect a good cry, enter in, and then recover as if nothing happened. For my part, I don't expect it, I don't willingly enter in, and my recovery is a hot mess.

Now, with that noted, it's the usual "end of year" things for my kids, but more specifically, it's the end of *a lot* of things for my high-school-senior twin boys, and with that comes the graduation, the open houses, the last lacrosse game of the season, Senior Day, Senior Night, Senior Award banquets, Senior this and Senior that—the speeches, the slide shows, the videos, you know the drill. And honestly, that stuff doesn't make me cry.

It's you people.

Yeah, that's right. *You* people. It's all your fault.

You come up to me and tell me what nice boys I have. You really mean it, or maybe you're just being nice yourself, but the truth is, I agree with you. I *do* have nice boys and I want you to keep telling me these things, even if I don't expect it.

What you don't expect from *me* is that as soon as those words come out of your mouth, I'm on the verge of crying like a little baby.

I want to reciprocate and tell you how much I appreciate you and your kind words and how nice your kids are too, but instead I'm left mumbling something unintelligible, walking the other direction so you won't see me catching my breath as my chest heaves uncontrollably.

I can no longer compose myself.

Just this past weekend, a friend and mother of another lacrosse player came over to me at the end of (you guessed it) their last high-school lacrosse game *ever*, where testosterone and all things manly had just been on full display, with boys hitting each other with big sticks and bravado on their pseudo-battlefield. She walked over and gave me a hug and said she'd been emotional about it being the end of the season. That triggered it a little—you know, *her* crying. But then she just had to say it.

She told me what great boys I had and how much they'd be missed next year.

Couldn't she have said the exact *opposite*, so I could go and smack them? "They did *what*?" I'm used to that emotion.

But no, with her sweet words, just like that, my unsuspecting friend pushed me over the edge of the cry cliff. I looked up at the trees as I fell, and I thought of the perfect excuse: *Can you believe all these trees are blooming at once?* Would she buy it? My allergies *are* bad this time of year.

Oh, who am I kidding? It was too late. Once again, the sharp inhale of my masculine exterior exhaled as a gush of raw emotion. Right then and there on the sideline, around a bunch of high school lacrosse players, I became a softy.

I've tried to figure this out—you know, what's behind this sudden show of sentiment. I tend to look deeper than just the obvious, and I'm concluding that it might have more to do with, well . . . *community*. It really *is* you people. In many ways, we're all in this together, but I tend to build up walls and not let others in. For eighteen years Kristie and I have been working on these *projects*, and we can't allow anyone to see the final version until they're ready. We can't let you see what it takes to raise nice boys who are worthy of your kind words because behind these walls, it's pretty messy. Really messy at times.

Sure, we let them out to make appearances, every day in fact, but then we realize *whoa, that didn't work* and we still have enough time to bring them back in, behind the wall, to correct this or that, and send 'em back out for another day, and so on and so forth, until days turn into weeks and months into years and all of a sudden we've been working on these projects for a very long time.

But we can't put it off any longer. The walls are coming down. Or in my case, the floodgates are opened. Whatever you want to call it. *Here they are.* We've done the best we could.

And then you tell us, in so many words, "Well done."

That's why I'm crying. And because of that, I want to say thanks to all of you for your sweet words. I'm sorry if I turn into a mess right in front of you. But it's not my fault.

It's you people.

CHAPTER 29

Dear Future Wife of Levi

Dear Future Wife of Levi,

I'm like a broken record, I know, but I've been praying for you. I should be praying for myself too, because when you steal Levi's heart away, I'll be losing one of my steady companions. Out of my four kids, he's been the one who has lingered the longest in my company, like at the dinner table, eating slowly, willing to continue conversations and simply take his time. He seems to enjoy being with me, which isn't easy to come by, I know. He's watched countless football games with me and serves as my statistician and constant fact-checker when any question should arise. He apologizes if he has to leave a game early or go do other things—those very things that should be diverting his teenage attention in the first place.

Levi doesn't look a thing like his twin brother, but by now you know they have a special bond. It's not a strange twin thing where they wear the same clothes on the same day or feel the same pain; nothing like that. They just complement each other in a way that's become a pleasant surprise. As I type this, they want to be roommates in college, which is pretty cool, I think.

Speaking of college, maybe you'll meet him there. That's where

I met his mom. I knew she was the one for me the moment I laid eyes on her. I wonder if that's what will happen with you? Perhaps you'll pass by him in a hallway or be introduced by a mutual friend, or you'll be coming around a corner, carrying too much in your hands, and you'll drop some of it and he'll be there to scoop it up, and you'll laugh together for the first time. He'll scoop you up too, right then and there.

Your future husband has a lot of qualities I wish I did at his age. He's fearless in a way that I don't understand. I wonder how different my teenage years could have been had I not been apprehensive, indecisive, and well . . . afraid? Levi is not afraid.

I think you'll love how he's quick to seek out the party. He likes to dance and laugh and have a good time. Levi is also somewhat, shall we say, *unconcerned* with the details. It's not a clueless thing or an obliviousness as much as it's just a calm and steady approach toward all that's coming at him. He's the embodiment of *chill.* Somehow though, he still keeps an eye out for how he can help, especially when others aren't feeling that calm. Others like his parents.

Levi is quick to chip in with us. He anticipates stress and tries to undercut it. He's had a lot of practice. I think you'll love that about him in your marriage because he'll see it coming. He'll forge ahead of it and find a different path for you, maybe one with better scenery. This is good because marriage is a marathon, not a sprint, and he'll run right next to you. Yes, you're the fortunate one now, because you'll have him as *your* steady companion.

Now don't get me wrong, it's not all roses with Levi. He's been in his share of trouble. He can also be critical, so you'll need to help him there. I pray you'll have a natural ability to offer grace toward others so that he watches and finds himself doing it too, without much effort, like he's picked up a good habit along the way.

Levi is the smallest of my three boys, but the scrappiest; he's willing to stare down anyone and defend himself or his friends when necessary. He doesn't care that he's smaller. His light blue eyes transform into something like violet when he's sensing a threat. I've seen it. I wish I could be there the first time they grow dark in defense of you. He won't think twice about it, if you're wondering. Chalk that up to playing football and lacrosse and many, many years of proving his mettle with two older brothers.

I tell the story a lot about when Levi was born. He's probably told you too by now, but he didn't have a very good view of it like I did. It was an emergency C-section delivery and I watched the whole thing. He wasn't alive when he was finally pulled out, limp as a dead fish. I never want to see that color green again—that greenish death pall—in any form. After he was revived, he ended that day with all sorts of tubes and wires coming out of him, and I remember thinking he looked mad about it. Thankfully he made his way through all of that and has grown into the man you will call your husband.

I'm excited to meet you someday, future Mrs. Jacobson. Ours is a family full of love and loyalty. We've learned to hold each other close through the ups and downs of life, like we're on some kind of roller coaster grasping hands in between the cars. We'll gladly invite you onto that coaster with us. It's exhilarating, and you might lose your breath here and there, but we've got you. Just grab on.

Speaking of roller coasters, Levi has always loved them. He wanted to ride them long before he was tall enough. When he was finally able to, he rode the highest and fastest without even a hint of apprehension. It's that fearless thing again.

I guess I should wrap this up now, so just let me say how grateful I am for you. I'm blessed to know that you're in his life. Just as God intended, you will become one with him, and it's that oneness that will surprise you and overwhelm you and maybe even show you a glimpse of heaven.

Just one more thing, if it's okay. Do you mind if I borrow him from time to time during the football season?

CHAPTER 30

Circles Are Good

When you started to crawl, you'd chase each other in a circle on our family room floor. One would tackle the other, and you'd both laugh, roll around, and do it all over again. I wish I could have stopped time, right then and there, but no such luck.

Then you learned how to walk, and soon you were running around the house, chasing each other in a bigger circle, through the kitchen and living room, then the dining room and back again. A circle was good because you'd come back around.

We taught you how to ride your bikes, remember? You stayed in a circle for that too: our cul-de-sac. A big evergreen tree in the middle of it shielded you for a moment, until you'd emerge, mops of blonde hair in the wind, still chasing each other, leaning into turns and picking up speed.

But then, before long, you veered out of that circle. You made a beeline to explore and find your friends. That's okay, it was just our neighborhood. You'd ride from house to house and back again. A bigger circle now.

We took leave of our senses by teaching you how to drive and by helping you with your first car. Freedom called, and you didn't need us anymore to take you places. More friends, and some of them girls. You drove in circles around our town, still from house to house, but now to school, football and lacrosse fields, maybe a party or two, in a loop that always brought you home.

So now you're getting ready to leave for college. You've got a lot of nerve, veering off at the same time. It's going to be hard enough saying goodbye to one son, but two? Seems you were just chasing each other around in diapers on the family room floor. I really wish I could have stopped time, right then and there.

But no such luck.

It's okay. Keep at it. Head out in a beeline to explore and find more friends. It'll be a mighty big circle now, I guess, at a campus, leaning into turns and picking up speed, out into a state, a country, even a world. Just do your best to keep it a circle.

Because circles are good, and you'll come back around.

CHAPTER 31

Smiling While Inside I'm Not

So the time has come. I can no longer busy it away, feigning some project, working on this or that, hoping that summer will last a bit longer or that I'll wake up back in 2005 when I was defined by your need of me. I will now join the legion of parents posting pictures of a dorm room, with comments like "their new home" and "the next chapter." I will stand in that crowded space smiling while inside I'm not. I will encourage your new surroundings, share hugs, feign distraction, look for the exits, and wish that fall break would get here already.

Being your father has been identity forming. Of course, it's been book-ended by being the father of your older brother, through whom I found the bravado I was lacking, plus some sympathy at various points while he weaved himself in and out of trouble; but he emerged into that tough exterior, and I suppose I did too with my vicarious adoption into the Marine Corps, where I've enjoyed the fruit of raising someone so dangerous, so full of energy and strength.

I am also the father of your sweet little sister, through whom I identify as a protector; some sleepy sheepdog with one eye on the wolf, crafting my designs to thwart, defend, and destroy, all the while gently tending to the helpless sheep I make her into.

But I suppose as your father, twins in the middle, I claim some street cred. It is because of you I received the inevitable awe and wonder: "Wow, you were busy" or "How did you do it?" or "I could barely manage the two I had, and you had four?" Yes, through you two I achieved some godlike, mythical, and wholly undeserved attribute as a super-father who managed to juggle it all against the odds.

Honestly, I don't remember much about my identity before becoming a father. After you two came along, I said goodbye to what identity I had left and probably wouldn't recognize myself, back before responsibility was heaped upon me and before I took the time to calculate what it would mean. I'm not sure I ever calculated it. I jumped into the rushing rapids of it all because it looked like fun.

And yes, this week I suppose the rapids will slow to a babbling brook, some tributary off to the side because I will leave you off and let you go, not feeling very godlike, wondering if I did it well, or even right.

I tried not to show too many of my weaknesses. I know I was often the immature parent, the joke maker, the yes-man, and the peacemaker. Did I laugh when I should have held back? Better yet, did I cry enough in front of you?

I wonder if I took my faith seriously enough. Did I lead by example and teach you about love and serving others? I wonder if I loved your mother well so that you'd someday follow my example. I wonder if I listened to you intently at the right time. I wonder if I taught you the way a man sometimes must balance work with the good stuff outside of work. The best stuff. I hope I showed you the right balance.

I didn't teach you how to change the oil in your car, or how to tie a good knot. As to the changing of the flat tire, I barely knew how to change one myself, so I'm not sure I could teach you that.

I didn't teach you how to fish or hunt. I didn't teach you how to build things, because I didn't know how to build things. I taught you how to laugh at how bad I was at building things, or fixing things, or using tools in general.

I taught you a firm handshake, a good look-in-the-eye. I taught you to speak up. I taught you about making family a priority, how to react and be slow to anger, and how to adapt. I know I taught you about forgiveness.

I certainly showed you what it looks like to be the center of stories. The very ones I love to write about you.

Maybe there's no getting it right, this fathering thing, but just to lean in the direction that's good and honorable and decent, and pray some of the best seeds of wisdom I offered will take root along the banks of those rushing rapids.

As I leave you off and let you go, please know that I'm very proud of you two and can't wait to see where life takes you in these next four years. I hope I taught you the things you'll need along the way to become the best version of yourselves.

Without a doubt, being your father has been identity forming, but I could never have imagined a better one.

Part Four

The Fourth Child

She insists we dance.

CHAPTER 32

Sometimes All at Once

I watched you dance last Sunday. You should know that I grumbled a little about the cost to get in, mostly because it took me by surprise. It seemed like a lot for a dance recital, especially since I already had to pay for everything else—you know, the costumes, the makeup, and the lessons.

So I told your brothers to get out of line and wait in the lobby because I wasn't going to pay for them to sit there and fight and make fun of all the dancers, or most specifically, you. I can get that for free at home.

I forked over the cash and went in with your mother and your grandparents. A few minutes later, we all looked to our left and your brothers, the very ones I had just told to wait in the lobby, were sitting in another section, casually eating from a bag of chips like they were at a movie. They sneaked in without paying, which made me mad and embarrassed and, at the same time, a little proud of their resourcefulness.

Fathers have these feelings, sometimes all at once.

And this is really what I'm getting around to, those feelings all at once, because I wasn't really prepared for what happened next.

You see, I don't like to be ambushed by emotion. I need to ease into it, discover it, analyze it, and let it out in manageable pieces and parcels. If I do sense such an ambush is coming, I've trained the muscles in my face to contort and then I clench my jaw and teeth in such a way that I can, in almost a superhuman fashion, fight back tears.

It's a gift, really.

And so, my eyes were still focused in a steely gaze on your delinquent brothers, when suddenly the lights went down and the music started. After some up-tempo dances, someone thought it would be great to choose songs that already tugged on my heart-strings, and then add in the power of dance. I didn't think that was very fair at all. The beauty and the art of it was simply, uh . . . overwhelming. It was, in fact, a perfect storm of emotion.

With each dance it got worse; relentless, really. I had no time for my face contortions. No time for my jaw clench. I sat there emasculated, tears forming these ridiculous pools in my eyes, and then they started to roll down my cheeks, and that hasn't happened since the mid-'70s. Pretty much everything got all blurry because the dances wouldn't stop and the tears wouldn't stop, and I felt all vulnerable and exposed, even sitting in the dark.

It wasn't just an ambush. It was a sneak attack.

Your mom looked over and asked that dreaded question that no man wants to hear: "Are you crying?"

I shifted in my seat and turned my head a little to cover my girly-man shame. I tried to put my finger in the dike as best I could, but it was too late. I thought my dad might reach for his hankie. Yes, your grandfather still carries a hankie.

And all of this was going on before you even got on stage. That part really wasn't fair.

I had nothing left at this point, and you came out from behind the curtain, very lovely, just a perfect miniature of your mother beside me. There were a lot of girls up there, but to me, you were the only one. There was this radiance about you, nearly a glow. I wondered if anyone else saw it or just me, but your smile lit up the stage. As you can imagine, I had pretty much given up on holding back the tears.

I think even your brothers, the criminals, were a little taken aback. When I looked over at them, they were all at once still, their eyes glued on the stage.

I know you'll roll your eyes at me, but you've grown up to be such an exquisite, graceful, and talented young lady. I'm so very proud of you. There are these three boys ahead of you, and I love them like crazy but they're physical and tough and they wrestle and break things. They shoot each other with their BB guns. They sneak into places without paying. They don't smell nice like you. They outnumber you three to one and they still pick on you. You're like this peaceful, beautiful little flower that somehow broke through rough, trampled ground.

So anyhow, yes, it's true. Your dad cried a bit on Sunday. You probably don't see that as often as you should. Here's another thing you should know: it was only $10 a person to get in, but it was worth every penny. I would have paid anything to stop time, right then and there.

P.S. Dear K. Monique's Studio of Dance: That was a great recital. And yes, I know I owe you more money.

CHAPTER 33

Dear Future Husband of Chloe

Dear Future Husband of Chloe,

I don't know who you are. The law of averages would suggest that right about now you're twelve or thirteen. Maybe you live here in Indiana or halfway around the world. You could be an athlete or a geek; you could be right-brained or left. Musical, maybe, or not so much.

Whoever you are, you should know that I've been praying for you, for a variety of reasons. If you've felt a strange sensation, that's probably God preparing you for what's in store. I found out that my wife's parents prayed for me when she was still a baby. It blows my mind, but, yes, strangers were praying for me just like I'm praying for you.

So, here's the thing: You will see my daughter for the first time and you'll fall in love, just like I did. Trust me, I know. I'm probably a little biased, but she's quite stunning. Her brown eyes will draw you in, and you'll lose all ability to speak. Love does that sometimes.

Setting outward appearances aside, you'll find out that she's even more beautiful on the inside. God gave her a heart full of love and compassion. She's patient and she's kind and she has a great sense of humor. She dances all the time and she loves life. Once you get to know her, your life will never be the same.

But quickly back to outward appearances. You'll want to take a look at her mother, because by the time you meet Chloe you'll have heard that most women turn out looking like their mothers. It might take a while, but sooner or later, the saying comes true.

You'll be thanking God she looks like her mother. Trust me on that one too.

Truth is, I've had people come up to me for years, ever since Chloe was a little girl, to tell me I should *watch out*. Better lock the doors and the windows, they'd say. Better get 'round-the-clock protection for her because she's gonna be a looker! At first I thought they were just being nice, but I don't think that anymore because, well, suddenly, she is a looker.

She'll have plenty of protection, even after you're in the picture. I'll get to that in a minute.

To be honest, I'm a little jealous of you right now because I know you'll steal her heart away. I pray you'll know what an amazing gift you're receiving. It's all backward and upside down because I don't even know you yet, but in ten years or maybe fifteen, I'll have to give her to you. I can't believe you'll get to spend more time with her than I will.

As in, the rest of your life.

Now as to the "rest of your life" part, I hope you know that's nonnegotiable. Don't be getting any funny ideas in your head someday about "options." You need to go into this knowing that yours will be the one in two marriages that ends in marriage.

Here's another thing I pray (and it may sound strange): I pray that your father is head over heels in love with your mother, that you see examples of it every day, and that you know it to be a true love, deep down inside where your feelings go. I hope your dad isn't shy about it, and that he's ever attentive to your mother's needs, and that you're taking mental notes. I pray that he's "all in," for better or for worse.

Actually, those are your only options, son. You get "for better" or you get "for worse." Sometimes they come so close together that you want to pull your hair out and leave. But leaving isn't what men do. Either way, I pray it's always worth it, and that the "for worse" part serves to grow the love you have for my daughter, so that the "for better" stuff is that much sweeter.

It's important that you know that Chloe is going to expect you to love her in big ways. Sorry, kid, but I'm blazing a trail for you to follow, so you better get used to that. God knows I'm not perfect, but my daughter knows I love her, and she knows without a doubt that I love her mother with abandon. Speaking of God, I'm praying like crazy that you'll love Him with all your heart, soul, and mind. I pray you'll love Him more than Chloe, because this is just how it needs to be to work best.

Trust me on that too.

You're young now, but God knows no boundaries of time. Right now, He sees you as the man that Chloe will love. Yes, He knows that man already. He knows the day you'll first pass by her or see her out of the corner of your eye. I wonder if it will be in a hallway—or maybe at a dance? Did I mention that she loves to dance? Maybe it will be outside by a tree or in a park, or you'll see her walking down the street. All I know is that when you do, you'll lose part of your heart, or even all of it.

Don't forget that she's afraid of thunderstorms. You can't ever make fun of her or treat it lightly. Just hold her tight and get her through it.

There's another thing I want you to know: I'm praying that you're honest with me when you ask for her hand in marriage. I plan to take you by the shoulders and look you in the eye and make sure you're ready. If you're not, that's fine. Take the time you need to make sure. If it's *never* the right time, then I guess this letter is for someone else.

I need to break away from all the nice and encouraging words, if only for a moment. Should you lie to me about the commitment you're making to my daughter, or treat it lightly, there's something else I pray for: I pray that you're in great shape, and that you can run really, really fast.

You know that feeling I told you about before? That strange sensation you now know was me praying for you? This isn't that feeling. There's another sensation you might get, sort of like goose bumps or the hair on your arms standing up. Maybe a sudden chill in the room. I hope you never forget what that feels like. That's exactly what you'll feel the first time you find out that Chloe has three older brothers.

You see, I mentioned the thing about getting in shape and being a great runner because you'll need to be if you should choose to harm their little sister in any way. Chloe's oldest brother is a U.S. Marine, and the other two play football and lacrosse and really seem to like physical contact. You'll need to run fast, and far, and find a really good place to hide, because, well, the Marine is the one who really has a special place in his heart for his little sister. By the time you're in the picture, he'll probably have a collection of guns that he likes to take apart, clean, and keep ready, and he'll have honed and perfected a certain set of skills. Plus, he'll have a lot of friends who are also Marines, and they really like to stick together (if you haven't heard).

Wow, sorry for that little sidestep there. Seriously, my prayer is that you really are "all in," and if so, you've got nothing to fear. Look on the bright side: with three brothers, she'll already *get* you. She'll have lived most of her life with guys. That's a head start on understanding what makes you tick, and marriage needs all the head starts it can get.

It will all work out. I'm going to keep praying for you from now until you arrive. We will love you as our fourth son, and you will have three new brothers. Did I mention one is a Marine?

Most importantly, you will have my daughter, the most wonderful gift I'll ever have to give away.

Trust me, I know.

CHAPTER 34

Still Be My Little Girl

You wrote a letter to me just prior to your eighth-grade graduation. I know the school made you do it, but I loved it all the same. Your brothers wrote similar letters a few years ago, but theirs veered toward the comedic. I wasn't sure what to expect of yours.

You should know that I got pretty choked up when I read it. Of course, I was sitting with a bunch of people waiting for the graduation to start, so I fought back any show of emotion. Somehow, in two pages, you expressed (for both of us) much of what was churning inside.

You suspected correctly that I'm a bit nervous about you moving on to high school, and so, with heartfelt reassurance and wisdom beyond your years, you used this opportunity to prepare me for what was yet to come. You did it gently because while I'm your father first, you see me as your protector; a guardian who has kept you under wraps for as long as I can—especially from boys—and that time might be coming to an end. I've heard it all before, and yes, I know it's right around the corner. Your mother has been warning me to ease up, but I still dread the topic, as most fathers do.

I will admit, though, it felt better coming from you, this subject of boys. You assured me that everything would be all right, because they're just friends, and that despite it all, you'd still be my little girl, the same one with brown eyes and freckles on her cheeks. I'll try to remember that the next time you and I are out in public, because I'm pretty sure the boys that come around don't see a little girl at all. They see what I desperately don't want them to, and they go to great lengths to see it again. I watch like a hawk as boys of a certain age (and grown men of all ages) do a double take. I've witnessed it all, from the subtle to the blatant; the quick glance to the stare. Anything to catch a glimpse of you. Sometimes I'm able to block their view so that they get a load of me instead, your bodyguard. "Keep walking," I warn with my eyes (I avoid saying it out loud, so as not to embarrass you).

But the thing is, I won't always be around to block their view. Even now, it's getting to be impossible. Like when you dance or walk on stage for an eighth-grade graduation. We're taught repeatedly to focus only on the inner beauty of a person, and I'm behind that 100 percent, but sometimes the outer beauty is, well, unavoidable. It's as if we're collectively enduring a cold, dark and cloudy day and suddenly the sun peeks through and everyone senses that there's some light and warmth, if only for a moment.

That's what it's like when you walk into a room.

And so, back to the boys. You explain in your letter that there will be more of them in your life, because that's just a natural progression of things with high school. I might even have to meet some of them before too long, but you assure me these boys— your friends—aren't bad people.

I guess I need to start softening toward them a bit. I mean, I do have three sons of my own (the very three who've given you the toughness and skills to defend yourself against the boys who *are* bad people). I can't forever place all boys under the same negative light unless I'm willing to put my own boys there. I know a lot of parents just like us are trying their very best to raise sons who will someday be worthy of a girl like you—one that brightens and warms a day, even with an imposing shadow of her father nearby.

You closed your letter by thanking me for writing moving stories about you, and for always telling you that you're beautiful. I hope you know that I do mean your inner beauty, which will always win out over the exterior (though in your case, the competition can be fierce at times).

And then you thanked me for always protecting you.

You're very welcome, sweetie. I wish I could do it forever.

CHAPTER 35

You Insist We Dance

It started out quite simply one night, when I was in a good mood, doing dishes of all things. I started to dance—that bad kind of dad dancing—to some Wham song that was popular when I was your age.

And then you joined in.

One song after another we danced until I was exhausted, but you were just getting started. Sheer joy took over, and maybe because of that moment, we dance often. Even when you know my mood isn't so great, or the day seems dark, or something heavy hangs in the air; even when you can tell I'm thinking too much about what needs to get done around the house, you *insist* we dance. You light up the room with your smile as you set up that wireless speaker. Sometimes you have to dance by yourself for a little while, waiting for me to come around to the idea, but you find the same set of songs we love, and pretty soon my mood is lifted and that something heavy hanging in the air seems to disappear as I join in.

And so it is, with your dance-insistence-way-of-living, Chloe, that I never fail to find sheer joy in you.

CHAPTER 36

She's Got a Way

They went back to school today. I tried to sleep through the whole production of it, but I couldn't. So I pulled myself together and pretty soon I saw her there, brushing her teeth.

You should know that I'd seen countless mock-ups of the first-day outfit, but in the end, she chose wisely and modestly. She was extra careful with the dress code because just like her mom, she's a rule follower.

She's just so beautiful. I swear some good-looking guy caught my wife's eye in late 2000 and it's been hush-hush ever since.

I used to sing to her, all Billy Joel-ish, about her *way*, not knowing what it is, but that I knew I couldn't live without her. I remember her little head on my shoulder. That fresh dry diaper and the smell of a long bath. I'd softly rub her back and lay her down when she'd fall asleep and I'd put my hand on her chest, just to make sure she was still breathing. I'd sing about her smile, and how it heals me. I'd try to sing the same song every night, long enough that I would be in her psyche, her being, forever.

These kids of mine, they're not supposed to turn into these big people. I found my identity in their weakness, in my need to protect and guide and shape them. I covered their small stature. I would forever stand in one place with the sun on my back to give them the cool of my shadow.

But they're bigger now. Strong and independent. They don't need me anymore.

I should go back to sleep.

And so it's *this* that leads to some middle-age wonderment. It's a crisis perhaps. It's what makes me and maybe you and every other forty-or fifty-something parent re-calibrate. Or drink. What is this thing I'm tethered to, and if it's not there anymore, will I ever stop drifting? Will I find something else worthy to anchor this boat? I don't want to float aimlessly in the wake of their . . . uh . . . *adulthood*. I've got to stay alert. I've got to be ready in case they need me.

Older brothers waited impatiently on the couch, listening for the end of the teeth brushing. They'd been ready for what seemed an eternity and had no tolerance for last-minute touch-ups and primping.

Finally, the reveal. The stunning bride on the Wedding of the First Day!

They left soon thereafter. No bus to walk them to, just a beater in the driveway that leaks oil and God knows what else. I watched them from the upstairs window as they drove away.

I should be worrying about them, but I'm not. Instead, I'm left worrying about what's next.

Part Five

MY FRIEND JIMMY

He possessed a natural courage that created a steady,
unwavering way about him. I remember, even as a child,
knowing that he would always be a leader
but at the same time a loyal and true friend.

CHAPTER 37

You Were a Memory Maker

Your mom walked up to me one day when I was in my driveway. She was dropping you off to play, and right about then we were eight years old or so.

She told me that some kids made fun of your shoes that day. You still had them on, and they had a pretty thick heel. They were brown, but sort of like sneakers. Back then, that alone was enough for mean kids to start in with the taunting and the bullying. You were innocent, of course, because how could you have known that you should only wear white sneakers, and that the *only* acceptable brands were Adidas, Puma, or Nike? I'll never forget how thankful your mom was that I hadn't made fun of them, or you, and how she told me right then and there that I was a true friend. She was concerned that it would happen again, and I wonder if she thought I was someone who might protect you. You also had a tiny bit of a stutter, so it could be she was sensitive to what kids might say or do, no matter what kind of shoes you were wearing.

I suppose it's possible after that day that I did usher you into a new group of friends, perhaps with some unspoken seal of approval, because to my knowledge you were never bullied again. And you didn't need my protection—of this I'm certain. In fact,

I'm not sure how those kids got away with bullying you in the first place. I don't think you stopped wearing those brown sneakers either.

You were the oldest in your family with a house full of siblings. You had a younger brother who was close in age, so you knew how to handle yourself in a fight. I would come over to your house and watch you and Mike beat the tar out of each other, casually, like it was just part of your day. At my house, I had a big sister who was kind and gentle, so I was pretty much the last person you wanted on your side in a fight.

It didn't take long before I was the one looking to you for protection. One day, at the basketball court in Veterans Park, you and I were playing HORSE or maybe one-on-one. Some big, gangly, six-foot-tall bully of a kid with curly blonde hair came over and took our ball, just because he could. You went after him like he was about three feet tall and you got our ball back. It had some blood on it from that kid's nose, and you wiped it off in the grass, passed it to me, and said, "Your ball."

One day we were in the Poconos and we were walking to a place that had a pinball machine. Some mean kid ambushed us and took all our quarters so that he could play instead. I told you to just leave it alone, because the kid was older and a lot bigger, but instead you waited around a corner and every time he put in one of our quarters, you ran up and hit the machine like it was a tackle dummy to tilt it and stop the game.

I could go on and on with stories, but I suppose the best way to describe you is fearless. You always were, and after your stutter faded away, that fearlessness was the main catalyst for adventures that comprise some of my fondest memories from both our childhood and teenage years.

I'm sure others who read this and had the privilege of knowing you will agree. After that brown-sneaker day, and the fleeting possibility that I may have ushered you into a new group of friends, let's just say you were on your own from there, as friends flocked to you and multiplied exponentially. In fact, you were still creating adventures for yourself and those friends well into your thirties. I was always happy to be on your side, because you were intensely loyal to friends and family alike. You were a memory maker, plain and simple.

Some other bullies who flew planes into buildings on a bright sunny day one September would ultimately cut your life short. You were innocent, of course, just like so many others that day. You never had a chance to set the injustice right, but others have for you.

Your fearlessness lives on, Jimmy, as best it can, in all of us and in the stories we tell. You were, in word and deed, the true friend, and a day doesn't go by without a hint of your presence in some memory, here or there. I even like to think you're still looking out for me, protecting me like you did when we were kids.

CHAPTER 38

He Could Have Been One of Us

Today is your birthday, Jimmy. Seems like a good time to let you know that I just made a trip to our old neighborhood.

I know it's a bit of a cliché, but the first thing I noticed when I turned onto Rocky Brook Road was how tall the trees had grown. They'd just been cut back, so they had this proud and majestic look to them as they towered over those seemingly untouched 1960-era houses from our childhood.

When I turned onto Millstone Drive, again maybe it was the trees, but I swear there was some type of holy peace that had settled there. It was so quiet and undisturbed. I drove toward my old house and, with luck, Scott, our old neighbor from across the street was out in his front yard. As I parked the car, I realized I might not be recognized, but I was, and he treated me like an impromptu guest of honor. His son Angelo was busy riding his bike, enjoying the safety of a road where few cars ventured. He could have been one of us, Jimmy, just a few decades ago.

When we were his age or a bit younger, we were always racing our bikes down my driveway. I remember my dad grabbing our handlebars, stopping us short, warning us to look left and right and left again. It was a good lesson, in theory, but maybe not a priority on that soft and quiet curve of a road along the Millstone River. To this day, it remains a fabled version of a cul-de-sac, maybe before such things came into neighborhood vogue.

I got a chance to go inside my old house. The current owners graciously invited me in to look around, so I walked through the remodeled kitchen and then out to see the backyard and the river and the roof we jumped from into the pool below, which has since been replaced by a koi pond. I looked at a backyard still filled with wonder and adventure: the hill we sledded on for hours, the meandering river with its nerve to keep flowing despite our absence, and the huge trees we climbed—the very ones with enough audacity to keep on growing.

Later, I met up with Rob and we drove down Rocky Brook Road and stopped to walk the long pathway into Veterans Park where we used to play tennis. Despite that bigger-than-life personality of yours and your easy way with others, I remember you were a very intense and competitive player. Rob was your doubles partner in high school, so he agreed. We reminisced about the time we had a party in the park and how those plainclothes cops showed up to join us. I'm pretty sure you were there, yet somehow you slipped away into the night while the rest of us were busy getting caught.

We drove by your old house and, believe it or not, deep in the backyard, behind a hedgerow, that crazy two-story fort with the cut-out windows and shingled roof still stands. I'd like to think that your dad is near you now, so please tell him he did a great job with the construction. It did look a bit sad and forgotten, belying the prominence it once held for us. It's funny because, these days, my kids think the best kind of sleepover takes place in the basement with video games and movies. But a perfect one for us was spent outside with a campfire under the stars, right near that fort, maybe with a stash of warm beers you swiped from your dad.

Anyhow, I was in town for our 30th high-school reunion. It was yours too. Photos were displayed, and there you were with

Eric and others in a memorial to lives cut short. You should know that you came up a lot in the conversations, perhaps because in the minds of others I'll forever be attached to you, at least from the early years. This is a good thing and a great honor for me but, all the same, I wasn't paying very close attention during the second half of your life. So, surrounded by these old friends, if I heard a new story about you, I soaked it up like a sponge. It gave me the privilege of knowing you better. You should also know that most people weren't remembering you as just some guy who passed on too soon. No, they spoke of you with a deep fondness and a wide affection, as if they too were forever at odds with why you had been ripped from our lives before your time.

As I drove back to the Midwest the next day, I got to thinking about how close you may be to everything, as if heaven is just across a border and not as complicated as we make it with our finite human minds. Maybe it's a little like the border I crossed on a country road between Ohio and Indiana—an invisible line with no fanfare, no suspicion, and no border patrol. I wondered this because you seemed to be such a natural part of my weekend, like the soft curve of Millstone Drive and the fort in your backyard, where the pieces of our childhood still linger unchanged.

I can assure you, Jimmy, that in our absence from that place and time, the memory of you has grown tall—proud and majestic, just like those trees. It towers over Cranbury Manor, where we each inherited a very special something that we nurtured in our time, and then had the privilege to pass on—to kids just like Angelo—perhaps some type of a holy peace that's settled there, where it's remained, undisturbed.

Happy birthday, Jimmy.

CHAPTER 39

Our Dads Were Just Fifty

It's that time of year again. You've been gone for a while now, but somehow, not at all. As usual, I feel this need to get together and get caught up, you know?

The war started right after you died. It's still being fought to this day, sixteen years later. I don't think it will ever end, to be honest, until the end of everything—the end of the world we know and that somewhat idyllic one we shared as kids.

Speaking of kids, you should know that I've nearly raised mine. Funny how sixteen years ago seems like yesterday. All that's changed for me from thirty-something to fifty is less hair and more weight and maybe some new socks, but for my kids it's been *everything*—from cradle to wonder to teenage angst and early adulthood. Sort of like the years we shared.

And yeah, I turned fifty this year, just like you would have. Can you even believe it? Our dads were just fifty.

Many of the stories I've shared with my kids have you as the main character, and with each retelling they become more legendary as I remember new details to embellish. Boys becoming teenagers becoming men are fueled by the antics of their father—for better or worse—so in no small way you were a part of their lives growing up. I think you'd be happy about that if you were still here.

My youngest, Chloe, was born right after you died, so she'll turn sixteen in just a couple weeks. It's interesting because her older brothers have friends who've noticed how cute she is, but they all steer clear to avoid a pounding. I'll need to talk to you someday about how you dated my cute sister without fear of a pounding from me.

Oh, that's right. You were fearless (I told my boys about that too).

I get to see pictures of your family on Facebook. That all came about after you died, the Facebook thing. I don't think you would have cared much for social media, but it's nice for me to see your nieces and nephews growing up.

I wonder if time stood still for you on that Tuesday morning, when life crossed over into a new kind of living, and now you exist outside of time in an eternal state of peace and joy. If so, it would be inconsistent for me to believe you know about the rest of it then, from late that Tuesday morning until right about now, because it was pure evil that took your life that day and a lot of others over the last sixteen years. Pure evil that has no place in the heaven you enjoy. Today that evil is spreading like a cancer that's metastasized, and it's rapidly changing our world for the worse.

Which brings me back to the end of everything.

I believe the end of everything will be the beginning of something infinitely better. And I believe you'll be there—you *are* there—to help me fact-check those stories that I've told my kids about you. Deep inside us there's a hope this will all get better in the time we have left, but it won't. We're like that runaway train with the bridge out in the distance, yet somehow we think there's still a chance for us.

Truth is, we were built to break and there's a lot of breaking going on these days.

I don't want to beat around the bush here for those who might be reading this. I think the hope we have is in the One who left that eternal state of peace and joy you're now enjoying. He knew all about how we were made to break, and He didn't like it at all. He wanted us to be with Him and to trust Him and then went to great lengths to prove He was trustworthy. I was there when you decided to put your faith in Him. I was the first person you told, and I'll remember it forever.

And thankfully, Jimmy, forever is a long time to get caught up.

Part Six

IF JESUS

If Jesus wasn't in my life,
this would be an altogether different book.
Probably not a very good one at that.

Because of Him, I've had more than enough.

CHAPTER 40

If Jesus Identified with Prisoners

It wasn't too long ago that my wife and I could be found corralling four little kids into the minivan, looking somewhat respectable and presentable for the twenty-five-minute ride to the building we called church. Just moments before, there would have been the crazed routine of breakfast serving, kitchen cleaning, refereeing, wardrobe selecting, hair designing, shoe tying, and the like.

About five minutes into the drive, I would look in the rearview mirror and marvel at how peace had settled over them. Maybe they were tired from the race to get out the door, but whatever the cause I'd be in awe of their little faces, the momentary calm, and the blur of beauty in the midst of chaos.

Truth be told, we usually listened to secular music on the way to church because I never felt like a father should be caught listening to one type of music on Monday or Thursday and another on Sunday. It felt fake and insincere and maybe a little desperate.

About halfway through the trip, sometimes we'd pass a group of convicts assembling at an informal staging area near the local quarry. It was a low-security chain gang preparing to pick up trash and serve a small portion of their sentence beautifying the highways and byways of our town. They wore reddish-orange vests as their scarlet letter, and a guard marched behind them with a steely eye and a scary-looking gun.

Meanwhile, Coldplay was waxing poetic about something or other as we passed the prisoners on that particular Sunday and, wouldn't you know it, my imagination raced ahead of me and the One we would worship that day was sipping His coffee and laughing with those very prisoners. Of course, He was fitting in like He always did, trying on one of their vests and identifying with them. I slowed the van, mostly out of surprise, because He always had a knack of showing up where I least expected Him. It was Sunday morning, for crying out loud. Didn't He have someplace *else* He was supposed to be?

I caught His eye as we idled by. No judgment was reflected there, no pretense, just a look of longing for me to join in, to get it, to do it, or maybe just learn from His example. It was a look reminding me that the healthy don't need a doctor.

Just like that, we were past them. I stared in the rearview mirror as the Jesus of my imagination and the prisoners He befriended started their march in the grassy ditches and the gravelly shoulder of the road. He went with them and helped them, picking up debris from some thoughtless driver. I could almost hear His conversation among them as He moved from one to the next, taking off His new orange vest and holding it up as a word picture or even leading an impromptu discussion along the side of the road.

I was a bit unsettled, as you might expect, by this altogether different blur of beauty in my rearview mirror. It's not that our destination wasn't a good use of our morning—you know, being among His followers, ensuring my children were taught about the Bible and worshiping Him, of course. It's just that there He was, picking up crap on the side of the road, a friend of prisoners, walking with them, befriending them, and talking about a different type of freedom. And laughing too, as if this were fun. Loving them, just as much as He loves me.

As I continued on my way that Sunday morning, respectable and presentable, I wondered about what church means—about crazed routines and perhaps chain gangs of our own making.

CHAPTER 41

If Jesus Held a Sign

A man was at the corner holding a sign. It read *Homeless*, I think, but it could have been anything. Maybe it was the *Will Work for Food* guy, or the *Need to Feed Kids* lady. It didn't matter, they're all *Down on My Luck*.

I planned to keep driving and avoid him, because of my usual charmed life, but the light turned red. No such luck this time. It was gonna be me and him, you know, in that awkward stare. I couldn't go forward and I couldn't switch lanes. I was stuck at the longest light known to man.

He walked to the window, unashamed. Guys like him are always fearless. My local news station did a scam piece not too long ago so that we'd all wise up to it. They exposed these people by following them from corner to corner with secret cameras, to vans parked in dark alleyways where they all gathered and counted their take. It's a pretty good racket, I guess. Of course, it's *all* a racket. As a matter of principle, I shouldn't give a dime to such a person because I'm just making it worse.

This time, however, guess who showed up? Yeah, He was standing there with him. Crazy how He does that, but He always finds a way. Of course, He looked like He fit in, like He was the long-lost friend of Homeless, or maybe even panhandling Himself? Some show of solidarity, I suppose. But He had to know what His "friend" was up to, right?

I gave Him one of those looks, but He didn't seem to care. He went over and picked up His own cardboard sign, scribbled on it and held it up to me:

You have a dollar in your wallet. Actually, you have three.

How did He know that? Oh, that's right.

He turned His sign around, and the back read:

Give it to him. He is ashamed.

What?

He twirled it around again. Same sign, somehow like magic, it had a new message:

I gave it to you. Now give it to him.

"But it's a scam," I mouthed to Him.

Another twist of His wrist and the sign read:

You don't know that. You think he wants *to stand here?*

He started turning that sign every which way like it was no big deal. I think He was showing off. Now it read . . .

He has dignity too.

Does he? I was planning on being part of the solution by *not* giving him something. *It's not right for the rest of us gainfully employed people*, I thought.

Why do you think you have a job?

Ugh. How does He do that and why does this light have to take so long? He shifted His posture a little, my imaginary Jesus. Sort of stood up straight and leaned toward the car:

That three dollars means nothing to you.

True, I guess. It's only three dollars. He keeps standing there all steely-eyed. He flips the sign again:

Three dollars connects you to him.

Oh.

And me to you.

One last turn of the sign:

I'll take care of the scam if there is one. You show compassion.

So right about then, I rolled down the window and I gave Homeless my three dollars. He thanked me with a big toothless smile as the light turned green. And I drove off, thinking a lot less about where my three dollars was going, and a lot more about my usual charmed life.

CHAPTER 42

If Jesus Knew You Were Paralyzed

The air is thick in your room and it feels like you might still be asleep, maybe in some continuation of a nightmare, because you can't get out of bed. You can't move, period. But your eyes are open and you're very much awake and this thing holding you back is quite real. It pins you to the sheets and molds you into some contour of an existence you've always known.

Something is paralyzing you.

Just like yesterday and the day before, there are some who know you and what it is that cripples you, and so they'll force your hand with a rousing promise that the sun will shine today, and it will pierce through every doubt that shrinks your body and your perception.

Day in and day out, you hear from these companions and they remind you simply to live and to muddle through it. And they tell you they'll help you see it through to the other side. But still, you know that the love of friends is merely a soothing balm—one that fills your cracked and bleeding skin, yet all too quickly it fades away.

True healing is always out of reach.

All the same, this morning they come again. Hands attached

to deliberate arms wedge in on every corner to find a grip of you. You'd fight them off if you had the strength, but it's no use. Sure, they understand why you're hesitant. Too many empty, unfulfilled promises have come and gone.

Still, they lift you up and out of bed, for this day bears a promise unlike any other. Soon your perspective is quite different as you're carried outdoors. They've heard of unspeakable healing, and, knowing what's best for you, you're now being delivered with a steady purpose toward *something*.

Your friends look down at you and they smile in unison, for they know *this* is it.

Finally.

The journey starts to get a little bumpy, and oddly enough, you're being lifted even higher as the voices around you start to intensify. You're in a crowd of people and some others join in to boost you over a ledge. All you can see is open sky and bright blue. There's talk of what to do next and some strange noises and maneuvering, and suddenly you're being lowered into a room. Some heated discussion is taking place—you can hear it as you enter—but your mere presence hushes the crowd. You feel awkward, intrusive, and out of place. At this point, though, despite the embarrassment, you're willing to try anything because, really, what have you got to lose?

The uncomfortable silence lasts only for a moment. Somehow, you're not at all out of place when you finally lock your eyes with His and He's the One you were meant to see. His face is kind and there's a knowing familiarity with everything that's been paralyzing you.

Desperately now, even though you've suffered with this for a lifetime, you can't wait another moment for Him to touch you and heal you. You'd reach up to Him if you could, but of course, you can't. This man with the beautiful eyes pauses and studies you as the crowd waits in anticipation. He draws in your friends to huddle over you. He tells them that He's overwhelmed by their boldness in seeking Him out, and their perseverance in finding a way through perceived barriers.

Then He kneels down to you, very closely now, and tells you your sins are forgiven. You're a little overwhelmed by His boldness and His way of doing things, the order of it all, for surely this was more about the healing of your body and this thing that cripples you, day in and day out. Instead, He's going straight for the jugular and some sin that lives within, that lies beneath, with your friends and every other conceivable person bearing witness to it all.

A murmur of whispers spreads through the crowd, for surely this man is doing the unthinkable. Silencing them, He tells you to get up and walk now. And so you do! Just like that, with your loyal companions beside you and tears are in their eyes for this day has been a long time coming.

Your muscles are weak from not being used, and so you'll need some help getting back home—and with what it means to live a normal, healthy life. Still, you can't keep from rejoicing, for you've been healed through and through. You, and those who would carry you, boldly came and sought the company of the One who keeps His promises and touches you and reconciles you to Him *first* before He gives you legs and feet to walk again. You smile as you embark on this new day, for others are watching and wondering how they too might walk free from the existence they've always known.

And so, indeed, the sun will shine today, and just like your friends promised, it will pierce through every doubt that shrinks your body and your perception.

Because *true* healing is never out of reach.

CHAPTER 43

If Jesus Used Three Words Today

I remember the story about when they came to get you. They came with six hundred very strong men just for you. Six hundred professional soldiers, to be exact. It was dark, so they brought torches and lanterns, just in case you ran away. They brought weapons too, for what I'm not sure. Maybe they had a hunch something was about to go down.

They just didn't know it would be them.

You asked them who it was they were looking for. They said Jesus. You emerged from the shadows and said, "I am He."

And those three words knocked them over.

Just those three words.

I missed this part, somehow, through Sunday school classes, youth group, college courses, and sermons about you. Six hundred soldiers leveled to the ground. Just moments before, hadn't they arrived en masse, armed with the power granted them by Rome and fully confident in their own training, skill, and resolve? And now they, to a man, were a heap of bewildered men, flat on their backs.

Six *hundred.*

Did their lanterns break? Did their torches go out? The mass chaos you created must have been a wild scene—seasoned warriors humiliated, scrambling and crawling on the ground, all looking for weapons in the dark as they tried to take up positions again. Anything to regroup, anything to save face.

Is there a reason I didn't catch it before, when I was younger and invincible and so accustomed to your other miracles? Is it because I'm older now, and more familiar with fear and trembling and responsibility?

So here I am. What masquerades as a battalion in my life that you would knock over? What sin, confident in its authority over me, would you render confused and humiliated in a chaotic heap on the ground? What else could you level with those three words?

I know you'd do it. Even today. You'd emerge from the shadows, and quite simply announce, "I am He."

If only I'd let you.

CHAPTER 44

If Jesus Went into a Bar

As He arrives in a town near yours, He is thirsty and perhaps hungry. And He looks tired.

At first, you wouldn't know it's Him because He's just like the others. So is His gait, His get-up, His rhythm.

Inside, though, through a dirty window with a tattered curtain, she sees Him. Drying shot glasses, she tightens up her apron string and stands on tired feet.

When He walks in, He goes right to the bar and takes His place on a stool. No one turns around because they couldn't care less. There's nothing to see. The back of His leather vest has some dried mud on it and His jeans need a good wash.

Or maybe they're just worn. His boots are beyond polishing.

She walks up to Him from behind the bar, and He smiles at her while she tells Him about the drink specials. *Just another one,* she thinks. *Same man, different day.* She's used to His type because they frequent this place, the corner dive, across the tracks on the outskirts of this and other towns. She readies herself for the abuse, the taunting, the longing, the quick pinches, and the empty promises of adventure that she's grown all too accustomed to.

He looks deep into her eyes and they're tired. She's wearing makeup from another day. Maybe yesterday, but she can't remember. Her skin is shadowed and bruised in places and her hair is pulled up, with strands that intentionally fall down her cheeks to cover and conceal.

But she's beautiful to Him.

She pauses for a moment and instead of looking down as she usually does, she locks eyes with His. He's not handsome in the typical sense of the word, but His face is very familiar. His smile brightens the room. His skin is dark or maybe that's grime from His travels, but it doesn't matter. She knows Him, but she's not sure from where. Or when. Or why. She's having trouble looking away.

All the same, He places His order and she reluctantly turns to go.

By the time she returns, He has already started talking to some regulars around Him. They're laughing, and He's graceful in His manner as He listens to them. So she just watches for a while from around a corner, feigning some duties.

When she finally approaches, He turns to her and His smile is still warm. She puts His order in front of Him. He slowly reaches for her tattooed hand. His hands are rough, as though He works with them, but His skin seems to form and mold into hers. Somehow she's aware that He knows the story behind every tattoo, every broken promise, every scar, and every wrinkle on her face.

She doesn't want to move her hand. He's not being flirtatious. Every instinct she has to pull away is gone, because this is the touch of the sober, kind version of her father's big hands. It is the soft warm skin of her trusting baby boy as he grips her thumb. It is the gentle assuredness of her big brother squeezing her hand tight and walking her through the halls at the new school. It is all of the good and true and right touches wrapped into one.

He says that He sees her pouring drinks and wonders out loud what it would be like to pour out something else. And to drink it in too—to quench a different kind of thirst and to know a different kind of life, one where the well never runs dry. Somewhere out there, out of the shadows and the long nights and the endless faces, is rest. And a safe place. It's something she hasn't known for a long time.

For some reason, with His hand on hers, in this dusty and dirty and grimy place, she believes Him. She's intrigued. She wants to know more.

So it goes, that when He stops again, maybe in your town, He may very well find that same grimy place where you hide behind a dirty window or a tattered curtain of shame. It's the corner dive on the outskirts of your hurt and your pain and your failure.

He's not prone to wait outside. He'll come right in, belly up to the bar, and smile. You can't shock Him. You'll want to look down and cover your scars and your tired eyes and your tattoos with stories behind them, but instead He'll grab your hand and you'll know from His touch that He has gone somewhere with you before. His face is so familiar.

And He's still pursuing you and promising to take you to that safe place. He keeps coming back as though He's known you forever.

And I suppose He has.

CHAPTER 45

If Jesus Calmed Our Storms

I know you had to sleep like the rest of us, but there's only one mention of it in all that's been written about you, and you were indeed sleeping peacefully at the time, perhaps dreaming about your home in all of its beauty and splendor.

Being who you are, though, you had to know that all hell was breaking loose just outside of those dreams, in the broken realm you chose to join. In your slumber, you were calm and still and relaxed, but they woke you, for they were in great distress. These grown men were accustomed to the sea and its rage, but they couldn't see a way out of this storm swirling around them. It couldn't have been the first storm they'd faced, so it must've been one for the ages. There on that boat, listing and swaying, they were gripped with fear, while those very same waves rocked you to sleep. The sudden brutality of nature overcame them and they turned to you like children frightened in the night. You already knew what they were feeling before they even woke you.

Helpless, really.

What you did next is something most of us already know about. You calmed the storm. The sudden brutality was no surprise to you. But what I keep missing each time I reread this is how you did it: You *rebuked* the wind. You scolded it like a petulant child. This wouldn't be the only time you would rebuke something that wasn't human. You would rebuke fevers and demons and even Satan himself.

But the wind? Well, that I can relate to because by my way of thinking, the wind is really the problem here. The wind is what causes just about every destructive storm we see on the news or experience firsthand these days.

And so, for me it helps to have a word picture, which I know you like anyway. There's a wind that's whipping up something fierce in our country. It is truly a storm for the ages, and I'm not sure how we'll make our way out without you. While you're no doubt calm and still and relaxed, many of us are in great distress. I know you're not sleeping because you're ever present, but I feel the need to wake you or at least remind you that all hell is breaking loose out here.

So please come and rebuke the winds of discrimination and still the waves of impatience and intolerance toward others. I pray that you'd rebuke the gale of greed and hush the churning sea of gluttony. Would you please rebuke deceiving squalls of lust and addiction, so that we can enjoy the calm waters of purity, sobriety, and grace? Jesus, please rebuke the forceful gusts of war and create rivers of peace. If there is a tsunami of scandal and deceit and corruption among our leaders, will you rebuke them and craft currents of Kingdom justice? Even now, rebuke the tempest of terrorism that is howling like a hurricane, and quickly usher in soothing streams of reconciliation among all nations.

That home you were dreaming about, with all of its beauty and splendor, well, we're dreaming about it too. Will you please calm this storm?

And He got up and rebuked the wind and said to the sea,
"Hush, be still."
And the wind died down and it became perfectly calm.
Mark 4:39 (NASB)

ABOUT THE AUTHOR

Jeff Jacobson was born and raised in New Jersey (exit 8 off the Turnpike), but he found his way to Indiana to attend Taylor University. For his day job, he is the Asst. Vice President of Claims at American Specialty Insurance in Fort Wayne, Indiana where he is fortunate enough to work with Major League Baseball teams and other sports and entertainment clients around the country. Jeff's oldest son Gabe (far right, above) is a Sergeant in the Marines and he has plans to attend Force RECON training in the fall of 2019. Tate (far left) and Levi are also attending Taylor, where they play NAIA lacrosse and yes, they room together peacefully (with the occasional insult when the opportunity arises). Chloe is a junior in high school and has plans to join her brothers and attend Taylor in 2020. Jeff stays engaged with Taylor by serving on its Alumni Council, and Kristie is really engaged because she works for Taylor as the Executive Director of Development. As you may have noticed, Taylor is something of a family theme here. While Jeff enjoys writing, he plans to keep his day job (because of those three kids who will soon be attending Taylor at the same time).

ALSO BY JEFF JACOBSON

So I Go Now: Following After the Jesus of Our Day

"I see him riding in on a Harley, the Jesus of my day. His hair is long and wild from the wind and it looks like he's been on the road for a while. But his eyes are still bright, and he smiles when he sees me. I guess he travels light because his saddlebags are mostly empty..."

Take a ride with a man who is forced to discover what a modern day Jesus would do; where he would go and what he would wear. Would he have tattoos, and if so, how many? What type of people would he hang with, and what might cause a scandal if he were doing it right here and now?

Experience a journey on the back of a Harley—a ride where faith and fiction collide with the non-fiction that sustains it; where imagination becomes wonder, and wonder itself leads to action.

ACKNOWLEDGMENTS

Many thanks to those who have helped me by reading drafts and with the overall editing process: Christy, Jenn, Jodi, Phil, Joe, Becky, Mom and Dad. Erik, thank you for an amazing book cover and overall design.

If you've read any of my essays over the years and you've encouraged me to keep writing, please know how much I appreciate you. I doubt this book would exist without your steady affirmation.

Most of all, thank you Kristie, Gabe, Tate, Levi, Chloe, Jimmy and of course, Jesus, for inspiring me to write about you.